HEALTHY HOMEMADE DOG FOOD COOKBOOK AND GUIDE

A Comprehensive Guide and 60 Nutritious, Quick, Healthy, and Mouthwatering Recipes for Meals and Treats for a Balanced Diet to Spoil Puppies and Adult Dogs.

BY JAMIE TATE

CONTENTS

PART 2

INTRODUCTION

Imagine being a dog and eating the same boring kibble every day. If you're lucky, your people may add a dash of warm water and a spoonful of pet minced meat to entice you to eat. You're left wondering why you don't get to partake in the wonderful aromas wafting from the kitchen when they make their dinner. In fact, you're told the delicious-smelling food is not for dogs.

Most puppies are weaned onto commercially made dog food as soon as they are old enough to need more than milk from their mothers. Many are scientifically formulated to meet your dog's nutritional needs, and most dogs thrive on such a basic diet. However, some dogs won't eat dehydrated dog food and others have a negative reaction to even the most expensive veterinarian-formulated pellets.

Of course, as a dog lover, you want what's best for your dog. If people are encouraged to eat less processed food free from additives, fillers, and preservatives, then surely dogs would also benefit from eating meals made from fresh ingredients.

You can't simply make an extra portion of whatever you're eating. Dogs have unique nutritional requirements and some human foods are not suitable for them.

Carefully planned, fresh, homemade meals, lovingly prepared for your dog, offer several benefits for your best friend's health and wellbeing. Lean meats, fish, legumes, a selection of dog-friendly vegetables, and a variety of grains supply a diversity of essential nutrients to keep your dog in tip-top shape.

It is critical to ensure that the meals you prepare for your canine friend are nutritionally balanced for dogs. Unlike humans who need a wide variety of vegetables in their diet, for example, a dog's gastrointestinal system doesn't require as much dietary fiber for good health, and too much could cause digestive discomfort.

Dogs need more protein and less carbohydrate and fat than people do. For dogs with special dietary requirements, homemade dog food ensures that you can avoid and manage conditions such as digestive issues, food allergies, and obesity. You can choose the ingredients most suited to your dog's needs and preferences, and, as an added bonus, homemade dog food often works out cheaper than mass production food.

Not only are the nutrients provided by the food you choose to prepare important, but you must also maintain high food-safety standards by taking the same amount of care when you cook and store your dog's meals as you do for your own food.

Dogs are notorious for eating almost anything they find in the trash, on the side of the road, or something they dig up in the park. That doesn't mean they have an iron-clad gut that is immune to food poisoning and spoiled food can still make them sick.

Some human foods contain nutrients that are not beneficial for your dog. Foods such as chocolate, grapes, onion, macadamia nuts, and some herbs and spices are toxic to your canine companion. Consuming such foods can result in anything from a simple stomach upset to something more serious such as kidney failure. Therefore, it is critical to do your homework and become familiar with the types of foods your dog can and cannot eat.

In the chapters that follow, you will find the answers to the most important questions about healthy homemade dog food. You will learn about your dog's nutritional requirements, how to create a healthy meal plan for your best friend, which foods to include, which to avoid, and how to transition your dog onto a fresh food diet.

To make it simple, there is also a comprehensive choice of practical recipes that will make your best friend's mouth water. Learn how to make tasty treats, hearty soups, protein-rich meat, fish, and vegan dishes your dog will love.

Even if you have a fussy eater, a puppy with allergies, or an elderly dog with a health condition, you will find the guidance you need to ensure your beloved pet thrives on a diet of homemade dog food.

Every dog needs love and a carefully crafted meal plan to ensure a healthy coat, strong bones and muscles, and shining eyes. Use the guidelines and recipes in this book to get your dog's tail wagging when you say: "It's dinner time!"

PART 1

CHAPTER 1
CANINE NUTRITION
BASICS

Good nutrition is the foundation of physical and mental well-being. This is true for humans and canines alike. The right nutrients in the right amounts support the healthy structure and function of your dog's body.

Commercial dog foods are formulated to ensure your canine companion gets all the energy, protein, fats, vitamins, and minerals they need. Unfortunately, the typical dog food pellets you buy from the grocery store or from your veterinarian are highly processed and contain fillers, additives, and preservatives.

Some pets have a bad reaction to the extra ingredients found in the food you purchase for them and others become fussy eaters with their owners trying one brand of food after another just to get their beloved furry friend to eat.

When you add special dietary requirements into the mix, such as a service dog who works in stressful situations, an elderly pet, or a dog living with a health condition, finding the right food can be challenging.

As a health-conscious human who loves their dog, you want to ensure that what you are feeding your canine friend is going to support them through all stages of their life.

For many dogs, commercially prepared kibble supports their needs and allows them to live a long and healthy life. However, if you feel the typical dog food is not meeting your dog's needs or believe they would be better off eating a fresh food diet, then you must become familiar with canine nutrition basics.

When you understand exactly what your pooch needs from the food you give them, you will be able to prepare wholesome meals that provide all the necessary nutrients and energy to ensure optimum health. Let's look at what is considered to be a healthy diet for dogs.

Nutritional Requirements

Dogs come in all shapes and sizes, ranging from the smallest Chihuahua weighing just 4-5 lb (1.8-2.3 kg) to an English mastiff tipping the scales at 200 lb (90 kg). Each dog has unique nutritional requirements based on their size, weight, and metabolism.

Other factors that determine what type of food and how much your dog should eat include:

· Activity level

· Life stage - puppy, adult, senior

· Lactating or pregnant

· Neutered or spayed

· Health status

Energy (Calories)

Once you have determined all the factors that contribute to your dog's nutritional requirements you can calculate how much energy or calories they need to consume per day.

First, calculate your dog's resting energy requirement (RER). This is the equivalent of a person's resting metabolic rate (BMR). It is the minimum amount of energy needed to sustain life. RER considers only how much energy the dog would need to cover basic functions such as keeping their heart beating and breathing.

Use the equation below to calculate your dog's RER:

RER = (Dog's weight in kilograms)$^{3/4}$ x 70 kCal/day

Example: If your dog weighs 15 kg (33 lb), the equation would look like this:

RER $= (15)^{3/4} \times 70$

$= 533$ kCal per day

In the next step, the RER is multiplied by factors determined by your dog's life stage, activity level, and whether or not they are neutered or spayed to calculate your dog's maintenance energy requirement (MER), the number of calories needed to work, play, and spin in circles when you get home from work.

Adult - neutered / spayed	1.6
Adult - intact	1.8
Adult - inactive or breed prone to obesity	1.2 - 1.4
Adult - needs to lose weight	1.0
Adult - needs to gain weight	1.2 - 1.8
Working dog - very active	2.0 - 5.0
Puppy - 0-4 months	3.0
Puppy - 4-12 months	2.0
Pregnant - last trimester	1.25 - 1.5
Lactating - week 1	1.0 - 1.5 (depends on number of puppies)
Lactating - week 2	2.0 (depends on number of puppies)
Lactating - week 3 and 4	2.5 - 3.0 (depends on number of puppies)
Senior	1.4

Example: If your dog is neutered and has an RER of 533 kCal per day:

MER $= $ RER $\times 1.6$

$= 533 \times 1.6$

$= 852$ kCal per day

Even if you master the complicated mathematics, the answer you get is still an estimate of your dog's actual calorie requirements. Your dog may need more or less energy depending on the breed. For example, although a Jack Russell Terrier is roughly the same size as a Maltese Poodle, the Jack Russell Terrier is more active and needs a higher daily calorie intake (Dog and Cat Calorie Calculator | OSU Veterinary Medical Center, n.d.).

If the math makes your head spin, you can use the values in the table below to estimate your dog's energy requirements.

Dog's weight	Average Daily Calorie Requirement Range (kCal)
5 kg (11 lb)	280 - 351
10 kg (22 lb)	470 - 590
20 kg (44 lb)	790 - 993
30 kg (66 lb)	1080 - 1346
40 kg (88 lb)	1340 - 1670
50 kg (110 lb)	1786 - 2444

WSAVA Global Nutrition Committee (2020)

> **Note on calories:**
>
> *1 kilocalorie is equal to 1000 calories.*
>
> *Your dog's energy requirements are expressed in kilocalories (kCal), which is quite a mouthful. Therefore, it is common practice to use the terms interchangeably. So, wherever you see the word calories we are referring to kCal.*

Now that you know how many calories your dog needs you can determine how much of each macronutrient they require. Macronutrients are the components in food that provide energy in the form of calories. They include protein, carbohydrates, and fats.

Research shows that dogs who are allowed to choose what they eat have a strong preference for protein and fat and very little interest in carbohydrates (Roberts et al., 2017). However, the macronutrient recommendations for dogs vary substantially between studies and the official *NRC recommendations (Rankovic et al., 2019). The average protein, fat, and carbohydrate requirements are summarized below:

- 30% protein (*NRC minimum recommendation = 8.8%)

- 40 - 60% fat (*NRC minimum recommendation = 12.4%)

- 10 - 35% carbohydrate (*NRC recommendation = 78.8%)

*NRC = National Research Council

Protein (The Building Block)

Protein foods provide your dog's body with amino acids, the building blocks of life. Twenty amino acids are involved in building and repairing tissues such as muscle, skin, and hair in both animal and human bodies. They are also essential for the structure and function of several critical molecules including antibodies, enzymes, blood cells, and neurotransmitters, making protein crucial for a strong immune system, digestion, delivery of nutrients, and brain health.

Of the 20 life-sustaining amino acids, 10 cannot be synthesized in the canine body and are considered essential nutrients. They include:

- Histidine

- Isoleucine

- Leucine

- Lysine

- Methionine

- Phenylalanine

- Threonine

- Tryptophan

- Valine

- Arginine

Different types of protein foods supply varying levels of each amino acid, and some don't contain the complete set. Therefore, the type of protein food you choose to feed your canine friend must be carefully selected to support the structure, function, and wellbeing of your dog's body.

Protein portion size:

Each gram of protein provides 4 calories. To work out how much protein to feed your furry friend, divide the number of calories they must get from protein by 4. So, our example 15 kg dog, would need roughly 30% of his calories from protein, or 64g of protein per day. If 30g of meat provides 7g of protein, we would need to give our dog roughly 270g of meat, fish, or poultry per day, di-vided between the number of meals they eat per day, to meet his protein requirements.

Animal-based proteins

Animal-based sources of protein provide a complete amino acid package. They also offer vitamins and minerals such as B-vitamins, iron, and zinc that are vital for your dog's overall health.

Lean meats, such as chicken, turkey, and beef are excellent choices to provide high-quality protein while keeping the fat content of homemade meals in check. Remember to remove the skin and bones of poultry before preparing your dog's meals. Small quantities of lamb, mutton, and pork can also be included in your furry friend's diet; however, it is advisable to trim excess fat off these cuts of meat to limit the calorie content and the amount of saturated fat your dog consumes.

Fish, such as salmon, mackerel, whitefish, herring, and flounder can also be a valuable addition to homemade dog food. Apart from protein, they are rich in omega-3 fatty acids, which promote a shiny coat and support joint health.

Eggs are another source of complete protein and essential nutrients, such as choline, which is used in the structure of cell walls and supports healthy brain and muscle function.

Plant-based proteins

Plant sources of protein generally contain starches, fiber, vitamins, and minerals. While there are a few plant-based proteins that provide all the amino acids, most are lacking in some of the essential ones, including methionine, tryptophan, and lysine.

Therefore, if you're planning a vegetarian or vegan diet for your dog, it is critical to include a variety of plant-based proteins that complement one another and provide all 10 essential amino acids to support your dog's health.

Legumes, such as beans, soy, lentils, and chickpeas are excellent plant sources of protein, fiber, vitamins, and minerals. The addition of grains, sweet potatoes, and dog-friendly vegetables can help ensure a complete protein profile in your dog's homemade diet.

The protein in quinoa supplies the full range of amino acids, making quinoa a valuable source of protein for your pet.

Carbohydrates (Energy Source)

The domestication of dogs has resulted in an adaption from a predominantly carnivorous diet to an omnivorous diet. When dogs naturally select their meals, they show a preference for protein and fat. However, modern canines do well with up to 70-80% of their calorie intake in the form of carbs, with the typical commercially prepared dog food providing an average of 30-35% of your dog's calories as carbohydrates (Rankovic et al., 2019).

Carbs are a source of energy for dogs, and provide 4 calories per gram. They also have important micronutrients and dietary fiber. While dogs don't have a requirement for fiber, including some in their homemade meals improves digestive health.

Note that it is not only grains and starchy foods that provide your furry friend with carbohydrates. They are also found in vegetables, fruits, and herbs.

Carbohydrate portion size:

The dog in our example, given 30% of his calories in the form of carbs would need 255 calories of carbs per day. Divide that by 4 to determine how many grams of carbs they need (65g). If half a cup of starchy food, such as grains or sweet potato provides 15g of carbohydrates, our dog would need 5 cups per day split between the number of meals they eat per day.

Fats (Essential for Health)

Fats are the last of the macronutrients, supplying more than twice the energy per gram as protein and carbs. Each gram of fat gives your dog 9 calories. Although fatty foods are calorie-dense, they are a critical part of your pet's diet.

Fats help the absorption of fat-soluble vitamins, A, D, E, and K, and form part of the structure of cell walls. Essential fatty acids, such as omega-3 and omega-6 fatty acids help control inflammation, promote healthy skin and coat, and support brain, heart, and eye health.

Fat portion size:

Continuing with our example, our dog would need 40% of his calories from fat (340 Cal). To figure out how many grams of fat they needs, divide the number of calories by 9, which equals 38g of fat. Remember that a large portion of your dog's fat is included in their protein foods and very little extra fat in the form of oils will need to be added to their meals.

Vitamins and Minerals (Supporting Vital Functions)

Vitamins and minerals are essential nutrients that must be provided by your dog's diet. They are involved in almost all bodily processes and deficiencies have significant consequences for your dog's health.

Table of Vitamins

Vitamin	Function	Sources
Vitamin A	Eye health, immunity, fetal development	Liver, egg yolks, carrots, yellow-flesh sweet potatoes
Vitamin B1 (Thiamine)	Energy and carbohydrate metabolism	Beef, pork, liver, legumes, wholegrains
Vitamin B2 (Riboflavin)	Supports enzyme function	Meat, eggs, leafy green vegetables such as spinach
Vitamin B3 (Niacin)	Supports enzyme function	Liver, kidney, fish, poultry
Vitamin B5 (Pantothenic acid)	Energy metabolism	Eggs, liver, whole grains, legumes
Vitamin B6 (Pyridoxine)	Supports red blood cell function, immunity, nervous system function, and hormone regulation	Salmon, tuna, liver, whole grains
Vitamin B7 (Biotin)	Metabolism of protein, carbohydrate, and fats	Eggs, legumes
Vitamin B9 (Folate)	Amino acid metabolism	Leafy green vegetables such as spinach, fruit, legumes
Vitamin B12 (Cobalamin)	Supports nervous system and DNA synthesis	Meat, fish, poultry, eggs
Vitamin C	Production of collagen, supports immune system	Sweet potatoes, broccoli, blueberries, strawberries, kale
Vitamin D	Bone health, maintains calcium and phosphorus balance	Beef, liver, fish, eggs
Vitamin E	Protects against oxidative damage	Vegetable oils, peanut butter, salmon, trout,
Vitamin K	Bone health, blood clotting	Beef, egg yolk, green leafy vegetables such as kale
Choline	Supports brain, muscle, heart, and liver function	Egg yolks, liver, meat, whole grains

Table of Minerals

Mineral	Function	Sources
Calcium	Bone health, blood clotting, nerve function, muscle contraction	Poultry, fish, dark green leafy vegetables such as spinach and broccoli
Chlorine	pH Balance, movement of fluid across cell membranes	Whole grains, meat, fish, sweet potatoes
Copper	Synthesis of connective tissue and blood cells, iron metabolism	Liver, fish, legumes, whole grains
Iodine	Production of thyroid hormones	Eggs, seaweed, fish, liver
Iron	Synthesis of red blood cells, energy metabolism	Red meat, liver, kidney, sardines, tuna, salmon, egg yolks
Magnesium	Muscle contractions, nerve function, bone health, enzyme function	Fish, liver, kidney, legumes, whole grains, cucumber, spinach, peas, bananas
Manganese	Enzyme function, bone health, nerve function	Mussels, seaweed, pumpkin seeds, liver, sardines
Phosphorus	Bone health, energy metabolism, pH balance	Eggs, wholegrains, legumes, fish, chicken, beef
Potassium	Muscle and nerve function, pH balance	Banana, sweet potato, spinach, apples, squash, cucumber, mango
Selenium	Antioxidant, immune health	Meat, fish, poultry, whole grains
Sodium	Fluid balance, nerve function, pH balance	Meat, fish, poultry, eggs
Zinc	Brain, skin, and eye health, boosts immunity, hormone function	Meat, poultry, fish, eggs, spinach, broccoli

Water (The Lifesaver)

Just like humans, dogs can survive a lot longer without food than they can without water. Therefore, you must ensure that your dog always has a source of fresh, clean water available.

Your dog's water requirements vary according to the amount of exercise they get each day, the environmental temperature, and her/his health status. As a general rule of thumb, a dog should drink 1 ml of water per kCal of MER or 1 oz of water per pound of body weight per day (Zanghi & Gardner, 2018).

Water helps to regulate body temperature, helps digestion, aids in the excretion of waste products, and is involved in thousands of biological chemical reactions.

Catering to Special Dietary Needs

The calculations in this chapter are geared toward the average pet dog. However, some dogs have special dietary needs and the amount of food you give them must be adjusted to help them grow, maintain a healthy weight, or help manage a disease.

Puppies (Growing Bodies)

For the first 3 to 4 weeks of a puppy's life, it relies on its mother for everything, including nutrition. The milk produced by the mother is rich in nutrients, and supplies everything her puppies need to grow and thrive.

Puppies begin to experiment with solid food at about 3 weeks of age. Like human babies, they need to eat small meals often throughout the day, and because they are growing rapidly, their energy requirements based on body weight are greater than an adult dog's.

To estimate your puppy's MER, multiply the RER by 3 for puppies younger than 4 months, and by 2 for puppies aged 4 to 12 months.

Senior Dogs (Changing Nutritional Needs)

As your dog ages, their metabolism slows down, they tire more easily, and they become more prone to poor health. As such, you will need to adapt your pet's fresh food diet as their needs change.

For example, if your elderly companion is less active than they were in their younger years, you will need to reduce the number of calories they eat every day to avoid weight gain, which can place extra strain on their joints or the possibility of developing diabetes. Multiply their RER by 1.4 to determine how much they should be eating.

Pregnant and Lactating Dogs

The duration of a dog's pregnancy, on average, is 63 days. Although the fetuses grow rapidly in the first few weeks of gestation, the mother generally only needs to increase her food intake in the final trimester (from 40 weeks).

Then, her energy requirements increase up to 1.5 times MER. Due to the growing fetuses taking up space in her body, it is recommended to feed your pregnant dog several times per day to ensure her energy and nutrient requirements are met.

Ensure that the mom is consuming enough carbohydrates to maintain a healthy blood sugar level and to prevent low blood sugar (hypoglycemia). You may need to reduce the amount of fat in her diet and increase the amount of grains, sweet potatoes, and vegetables in her food.

It is also crucial to ensure adequate intake of folic acid, essential fatty acids, calcium, and phosphorus. You may need to use a supplement for pregnant dogs to meet these requirements.

Once the puppies are born, the mother's nutritional requirements increase significantly. For the first week, depending on how many puppies are relying on their mother for their nutrition, she will need to eat up to 1.5 times MER. At 2 weeks, mom's requirements increase to 2 times MER, and for the third and fourth weeks, multiply MER by 2.5 - 3.

Just as human breastfeeding mothers must increase their water intake when they are nursing, so must your lactating dog. It is also beneficial for the puppies and the mother to ensure an adequate intake of calcium and essential fatty acids (Fontaine, 2012).

Weight Management (Maintaining a Healthy Weight)

An overweight dog is susceptible to the same health concerns as overweight people, including being susceptible to diabetes and heart disease. Therefore, it's important to ensure that your companion maintains a healthy weight.

Some breeds, such as Labrador Retrievers, are prone to weight gain, and you must keep an eye on how much they eat. For such dogs, the RER should be multiplied by a factor of 1.2 to 1.4.

Calorie intake must be controlled more strictly in overweight dogs to drop a few pounds. For these dogs, their calories can be reduced to the RER, or minimum energy requirement.

Summary of Portion Guidelines for Different Dogs

Steps to calculate how much homemade food to make for your best friend:

1. Determine your dog's size and weight, metabolism (are they prone to gaining weight), activity level (sedentary to very active), life stage (puppy, adult, or senior), health status, and whether they are neutered/spayed.
2. Calculate their RER.
3. Calculate their MER using the calorie adjustment factors.
4. Determine the number of calories for each macronutrient (protein, carbohydrate, and fat).
5. Calculate how many grams of each nutrient you need to prepare for your dog every day and divide the totals between the number of meals per day your dog eats.
6. Create a meal plan and get cooking!

CHAPTER 2
DIFFERENT NUTRITIONAL APPROACHES

Canine nutrition is complex and constantly evolving. While most dogs eat a diet of predominantly commercially made dog food, there are several other options for meeting their nutritional requirements.

As people become more aware of the health benefits of eating a diet suited to their personal needs and preferences, so they are becoming more mindful of the type of food that is best for their four-legged friends. As a result, a quick internet search reveals dietary guidelines and suggestions for every type of doggie diet from kibble to raw food, and from carnivorous to vegan.

In this chapter, we will explore the benefits of traditional dog food as well as how alternative diets can meet your best friend's nutritional requirements.

Traditional Dog Food Diet

The dog food you buy at the grocery store or from your veterinarian is formulated according to the minimum recommended dietary guidelines for dogs. In the United States, dog food is regulated by the Food and Drug Administration (FDA), and even the ingredients used in treats and chews must be officially approved by them or the Association of American Feed Control Officials (AAFCO) (*Pet Food | FDA*, n.d.).

You typically have 2 options when feeding your dog traditional dog food, dry and wet. Both are usually available in a choice of flavors, and you are able to select what you deem suitable for your dog's requirements.

Wet Food

Wet dog food is most commonly sold in cans or pouches and offers several benefits for dogs and their people:

- It has high water content, making it useful for dogs living in hot climates or those that don't drink enough water.

- Dogs with dental issues find wet food easier to eat.

- The stronger aroma of wet food is often more appealing to fussy eaters.

- Many wet dog foods are formulated to meet specific dietary needs for dogs with medical conditions, food allergies and sensitivities.

Wet dog food is not a good choice for all dogs, though. Some of the drawbacks of wet dog foods include:

- Price. It can be more expensive than kibble.

- It has a shorter shelf life once the can or pouch is opened.

- Wet food is often sold in predetermined serving sizes, making it challenging to control your pet's portions.

- It may contribute to the buildup of tartar on dogs' teeth as it does not have the teeth-cleaning benefits of dry dog food.

Dry Food

Dry dog food is sold as pellets, generally referred to as kibble. It is the preferred diet for millions of dogs, worldwide (Montegiove et al., 2022). The reasons for its popularity include:

- Kibble has a long shelf life. It can be stored at room temperature for extended periods of time.

- It is a convenient way for busy dog lovers to ensure their dog's nutritional needs are being met.

- A wide range of formulations are available to promote the health of dogs with special dietary needs, including weight loss, oral health, and diabetes.

- Many of the veterinarian-formulated brands provide nutrition tailored for specific breeds.

- Dry dog food promotes dental health. When dogs chew the hard food, it cleans the teeth by rubbing off any plaque and tartar buildup.

- It is a cost-effective way to feed your dog, especially if you have more than one dog or a large breed dog with high nutritional requirements.

Not all dogs thrive on tradition dry dog food and some of the drawbacks to consider when deciding what to feed your dog include:

- Kibble has a low moisture content which may be a problem for dogs with higher fluid requirements or those with urinary tract issues.

- Some dogs find dry dog food unappealing, resulting in picky eating behaviors.

- Not all dry dog foods are created equal. Some have only the minimum amount of nutrients and a lot of fillers. Learn to read dog food labels so that you can choose the best quality food you can afford.

Plant-Based Diet

With the rise in the number of people turning to a vegetarian or vegan diet for various reasons ranging from their health to the wellbeing of the planet, you may be wondering if such a diet is suitable for your furry friends too.

Dogs are traditionally meat eaters, however, through domestication their ability to digest carbohydrates has adapted to be able to effectively digest the carbohydrates found in grains, vegetables, and plant-based protein foods such as legumes.

The minimum recommended protein intake for dogs is 8.8% of their total daily calorie requirements (Rankovic et al., 2019), and it has been shown that dogs can thrive on a high intake of carbohydrates. Therefore, many argue that a vegan or vegetarian diet may be a suitable alternative for them.

As with any other type of diet for dogs, there are pros and cons of feeding your four-legged friend a plant-based diet. However, a meta-analysis of scientific studies concluded that a vegan diet does not negatively impact a dog's health (Domínguez-Oliva et al., 2023).

Another study that explored owner's perceptions of the effect of plant-based diets on their dog's health reported no health issues related to such a diet. Furthermore, fewer eye, gut, and liver problems were seen, and the dogs were reported to live longer (Dodd et al., 2022).

Benefits of giving your dog a plant-based diet:

- Environmental sustainability.

- It may help manage food allergies and sensitivities.

- It may help manage urinary tract conditions.

Possible drawbacks of giving your dog a plant-based diet:

- It can result in essential amino acid deficiencies.

- It can result in essential fatty acid deficiencies.

- Reduced intake of essential nutrients, such as iron and vitamin B12 may result in anemia.

Regular monitoring of your dog's health by your veterinarian is recommended if you intend switching them to a plant-based diet to ensure their nutritional requirements are being met.

Raw and Natural Diets

A growing number of dog lovers are choosing to feed their pets a minimally processed whole foods diet that includes predominantly raw or natural foods, especially meat, based on the ancestral eating habits of dogs. Such diets are referred to as raw meat-based diets (RMBD), biologically appropriate raw food diets, or bones and raw food (BARF) diet.

The meat is sourced from livestock or wild animals and can either be commercially prepared or prepared at home. The raw dog food you can buy at the store may be in the form of fresh, frozen, or freeze-dried meals. You can also buy premixes that must be served along with raw meat to enhance the nutritional value of your dog's diet with dog-friendly grains, vegetables and herbs (Davies et al., 2019).

Some of the benefits of raw and natural diets for dogs include:

- Makes it easier to avoid ingredients responsible for food sensitivities.

- Helps manage inflammatory bowel disease.

- Benefits lacking scientific evidence include improved digestibility and stool consistency, better dental health, and enhanced skin and coat condition. Some owners also report better health and behavior.

Due to the nature of the diet, there are some risks associated with feeding your dog a diet of raw meat and other animal products, including:

- It may result in an imbalance in calcium and phosphorus in the dog's body.

- Poor planning can cause nutrient deficiencies.

- There may be high levels of pathogenic bacteria present in the food.

- Splintered bones can be choking hazards and may cause intestinal blockages.

- It may cost more. High-quality raw ingredients can be expensive.

While raw and natural canine diets offer some potential benefits, most are anecdotal and not proven by scientific studies. If you choose a raw food diet for your dog, conduct extensive research, ensure that the food is stored and prepared according to strict food-safety guidelines, and regularly consult with your pet's veterinarian to ensure the diet meets your dog's specific dietary needs.

Weight Management and Caloric Control

Overweight and obesity in dogs is as much of a problem as it is in humans. It makes your dog more susceptible to health conditions including diabetes, heart disease, and poor joint health. Therefore, it is crucial to prevent excessive weight gain in dogs prone to being overweight such as Labrador Retrievers, Beagles, and Pugs. It is equally important to help your best friend lose weight if they already carry a few extra pounds.

For a dog to lose weight, the number of calories they eat must be less than the number of calories they burn every day. Therefore, their meals must consist of less energy, which is generally achieved by reducing the fat content of their food. To help them feel fuller and reduce begging, weight management diets for dogs have more fiber than regular dog food. To compensate for the reduced calories and nutrients, the food formulation may contain higher levels of protein and micronutrients to help maintain your dog's muscle mass (German, 2016).

Weight management diets must be guided by your veterinarian. They can tailor a plan to your dog's individual needs and monitor their progress to ensure the weight loss process is safe and effective.

Food Allergies and Food Sensitivities

Your dog may be allergic or intolerant to certain foods or ingredients used to make dog food. The signs your dog's immune system is reacting to the food they eat include itchy skin, paws, and ears, vomiting, diarrhea, hyperactivity, weight loss, low energy levels, or unusual aggression.

The first step in managing food allergies and intolerances is to identify what is causing the reaction. To do so, your veterinarian will put your dog on an elimination diet for a period that excludes all possible allergens including commonly eaten protein and grains. During this process, you must closely monitor your dog's symptoms to decide whether or not they are improving.

Once your beloved pet is no longer showing any signs of a food allergy, your vet will slowly start reintroducing foods to their diet. If there is no reaction to the reintroduced food, it is considered safe for your dog to eat, and if your dog reacts to it, you will have to buy or prepare foods that don't contain that specific food or ingredient.

To effectively manage food allergies, it is useful to make a habit of reading food labels on everything you give your dog to eat. By carefully managing food allergies and intolerances, pet owners can help their companions lead healthier, more comfortable lives (Olivry & Mueller, 2020).

Grain-Free and Limited Ingredients Diets

Typically used to manage food allergies and intolerances or to address picky eating, grain-free and limited ingredient dog foods can ensure your dog still eats a balanced diet. For example, soy, grains such as wheat and corn, or certain proteins can be problematic for some dogs and by eliminating them from their diet you can help alleviate common digestive problems and skin issues.

However, since the grains and proteins are replaced with other ingredients such as legumes, there are some potential problems with using such foods for extended periods. Research suggests that grains free diets may have the following drawbacks (Bakke et al., 2022):

- Using alternative ingredients can increase the price of your dog's meals, making it more expensive.

- Nutritional imbalances may occur when ingredients are restricted.

- Some research suggests a link between grain-free diets and dilated cardiomyopathy, a type of heart disease in dogs.

Homemade Diets

Health-conscious dog lovers may have doubts about the nutritional value of commercial dog food and the impact it has on their best friend's health and wellbeing, leading them to explore how to make their dog's meals from scratch, using wholesome fresh ingredients.

Homemade food may be the best choice for you and your dog. If prepared correctly, it offers your pet several health benefits. However, as with any other doggy diet, homemade dog food may have some drawbacks too.

The benefits of homemade dog food include:

- You have better control over the quality and source of ingredients when you select the raw ingredients for your pet's food.

- You can avoid preservatives, additives, and fillers by ensuring your dog eats only nutritious fresh food.

- You can tailor the meals to meet your pet's nutritional requirements and preferences.

- Food allergies and sensitivities are easier to manage as you can more easily avoid the ingredients that affect your pet.

A lack of knowledge and understanding of canine nutrition basics may be responsible for some of the drawbacks of giving your dog homemade food, including:

- Poor planning can result in a diet that is not nutritionally balanced.

- Nutrient deficiencies can occur if your pet's diet does not contain a variety of protein foods, dog-friendly grains, and a selection of health-promoting vegetables, fruits, and herbs.

- Dogs cannot simply eat the same meals you eat. Their requirements are fine-tuned and it is easy to overfeed them, causing nutrient excesses, especially fat, which may result in pancreatitis.

- It is time consuming to prepare homemade food for your dog. It requires continuous motivation and dedication.

- Homemade dog food can be expensive. Therefore, your budget must be considered before deciding to commit to a fresh food diet for your beloved pet.

The first step in ensuring that you feed your dog a balanced, nutritious diet is to understand your specific dog's nutritional requirements based on their breed, size, weight, and life stage. It is also crucial to know which human foods are healthy for dogs and which ones will make them sick.

The next 2 chapters will guide you in making the best dietary choices for your furry friend so that you can stock your doggy pantry and begin cooking mouthwatering meals for them.

CHAPTER 3
INGREDIENTS FOR WHOLESOME MEALS

As a health-conscious pet parent who is willing to learn about the complexities of canine nutrition and how to make healthy homemade food for a canine companion, you need a list of nutritious ingredients that can be combined to make mouthwatering meals and promote dog health.

From lean proteins and fresh vegetables to wholesome grains and essential vitamins, the ingredients you choose play a pivotal role in supporting your dog's health and wellbeing. In this chapter, we will explore the essential components of a nutritious homemade dog food recipe, helping you provide your four-legged friend with a diet they are excited to eat but also packed with the vital nutrients they need to thrive.

Dog-Friendly Protein Sources

As carnivorous animals, dogs are predominantly meat eaters. However, by living with humans and relying on them for their food instead of hunting for their meals, they have evolved to require less protein to meet their energy needs. A dog can get by on only 8.8% of their total daily calories from protein. However, the average protein content of most dog foods is as high as 30%.

The protein ingredients you choose to prepare wholesome homemade meals must have all the essential amino acids your dog needs to be healthy. Animal protein sources are complete proteins and are referred to as having a high biological value. Plant-based proteins are often lacking in specific amino acids and must be combined in a balanced diet to avoid amino acid deficiencies.

Lean Meats (Chicken, Turkey, Beef)

Chicken, turkey, and beef are excellent options for homemade dog food. Not only are they sources of high biological value protein, but they contain only a small amount of fat. On average, 30g (1 oz) of lean meat supplies 55 calories, 7g of protein, and 3g of fat.

Lean meats are also a source of vital micronutrients including iron, zinc, selenium, B-group vitamins, phosphorus, magnesium, and potassium.

Fish (Salmon, Tuna)

Most fish are a good source of protein for dogs. The main difference in nutritional value between different types of fish is the fat content. White fish such as flounder or cod are very low in fat with 30g (1 oz) of fish giving just 1g of fat. Dark fish including salmon and tuna are fatty fish that supply 3g of fat per ounce.

Apart from protein, the main benefit of fish in your pet's diet is the essential fatty acids they contain. They are rich in omega-3 fatty acids that help control inflammation and promote brain, skin, and eye health.

Plant-based Protein Sources (Tofu, Lentils, Chickpeas, Chia Seeds, Soybeans and Quinoa)

Although plant-based proteins can provide your dog with all the essential amino acids, extra care must be taken when planning a plant-based diet to ensure that their protein intake is balanced.

Tofu, lentils, chickpeas, and soybeans are excellent plant-based sources of protein, and they are generally well tolerated by dogs. Since they are legumes, they are also high in carbohydrates and fiber. It's best to transition your dog to a vegetarian or vegan diet slowly to avoid digestive discomfort from a sudden increase in dietary fiber.

Remember that legumes such as beans and chickpeas must be soaked in water before cooking them to reduce the cooking time and make them easier to digest. Half a cup (115 g or 4 oz) of legumes supplies 7g of protein, 1g of fat, 22g of carbohydrate, and 125 calories.

Chia seeds and quinoa are alternative plant-based sources of protein. Unlike legumes, they contain all of the essential amino acids, making them a source of complete protein. They are also a source of essential fatty acids.

2.5 tablespoons of chia seeds give 5g of protein, 9g of fat, 12 g of carbohydrate, and 140 calories. Due to the high fat and fiber content, it is advisable to limit the amount of quinoa and chia seeds in your dog's meals.

Nutrient-Rich Fruits and Vegetables

Dogs can eat a variety of nutritious fruits and vegetables. When they are included in their diet, it increases their intake of essential vitamins, minerals, and other health-promoting plant chemicals. Some of the best fruits and vegetables to include in your dog's diet are carrots, blueberries, peas, and sweet potatoes.

Carrots: Crunchy and Nutritious

Add some crunch to your dog's homemade meals with bright orange carrots. They may not be impressed by the color, but the texture can make their meals more interesting.

From a nutritional point of view, the orange color in carrots comes from beta-carotene, the precursor of vitamin A. It helps to boost the immune system, maintain a healthy coat, support eye health, and promote bone growth.

Berries: Nutritious

Another way of adding color to your pet's meals is berries. Blueberries, strawberries, blackberries, and raspberries make tasty treats. They are rich in potent antioxidants, vitamin C, and several other vitamins. These nutrients help to support the immune system and control inflammation.

Peas: Natural Fiber Source

While dogs don't need a lot of fiber in their diets, peas, both fresh and dried, are also a source of protein and carbohydrates, as well as several vitamins (A, C, and K) and minerals (iron, phosphorus, and manganese).

Due to their high fiber content, adding too many peas to your best friend's meals can cause bloating, gas, and digestive discomfort, so keep the portions small: 1 teaspoon of peas for smaller dogs and up to 1 tablespoon for large dogs.

Soaking dried peas before cooking them reduces their cooking time and may make them easier for your dog to digest. Fresh or frozen peas can be cooked without soaking.

Sweet Potatoes: Energy-Rich

Sweet potatoes are a starchy root vegetable that can be used as a carbohydrate source for dogs. They add a bit of natural sweetness to your pet's meals and increase the amount of beta-carotene, potassium, and vitamin C.

Healthy Grains

Grains can be a healthy source of energy, especially for active dogs. Half a cup of cooked grains (approximately 125g or 4.4 oz), such as rice, oats, corn, wheat, or barley contains 15g of carbohy-drates and 80 calories. Each type of grain offers a different set of nutrients with varying amounts of protein and fat.

Typically, grains are a source of vitamin A, B-group vitamins, vita-min E, iron, magnesium, phosphorus, and magnesium. Therefore, they contribute to your beloved pet's overall health and wellbe-ing by meeting their energy requirements and support skin, hair, and immune health.

Brown Rice: Nutrient-Dense

Brown rice is primarily a source of energy and dietary fiber for your dog. However, since the bran and germ remain intact, it also has a lot to offer in terms of nutrition. It contains small amounts of protein and fat and contributes significant amounts of vitamins B1, 3, 5, and 6, and a range of minerals including iron, magnesium, phosphorus, zinc, copper, manganese, and selenium.

Quinoa: Complete Protein Source

Quinoa is a high-protein grain that is rich in carbohydrates and essential fatty acids. A cup of quinoa provides 8g of protein, 39g of carbohydrates, and 3.5g of fat. It is an excellent choice for pets on a vegan diet as the protein it contains supplies all the essential amino acids to support the structure and function of their body.

The micronutrients found in quinoa also contribute to your dog's health. They include folate, vitamin B6, vitamin E, copper, iron, zinc, potassium, and magnesium.

Oats: Digestive Benefits

Oats is a carbohydrate-rich grain with moderate protein content. The grain contains a significant amount of water-soluble fiber which has proven to be beneficial for digestive health in dogs. It absorbs water in the gut, improving the consistency of your dog's stool.

Another important benefit of including oats in your pooch's meals is to slow down the release of sugar into their bloodstream and keep them feeling satisfied longer. Therefore, it is useful for managing diabetes and weight gain in pets.

Nutritious Fats and Oils

Your dog doesn't have a great need for fat in her/his diet. However, fats are a concentrated source of calories for very active service dogs or those needing to gain weight, for example. Most of the fat in your dog's diet will come from the protein ingredients you include in their meals and the carbs will contribute a small amount.

Fats are an essential part of your dog's diet and are needed to maintain the integrity of the cell walls, ensure the nerves are covered by a myelin sheath, and support brain, heart, and eye health.

Saturated fats found in fatty cuts of meat, such as the fat on the side of a pork or lamb chop or the skin of chicken and turkey have been associated with weight gain and pancreatitis in dogs. Unlike humans, dogs don't develop blocked arteries and heart disease from consuming too much saturated fat (Bauer, 2008).

It is still more beneficial to focus on healthy fats that are rich in unsaturated fatty acids, such as dark oily fish like salmon and tuna. If you feel your dog needs more of these fats in their diet, you can add some corn oil, flaxseed oil, or canola oil to their food.

CHAPTER 4
FOODS TO AVOID

There are many delicious foods and drinks that can be tolerated by the human body and its metabolic processes, and it is tempting to treat your dog with them. Unfortunately, the canine digestive system and detoxification systems are not as sophisticated or robust as that of human beings. As such, it is critical for your homemade food-eating dog that you are familiar with the foods and beverages they can't tolerate (Cortinovis & Caloni, 2016).

Human Food Toxic to Dogs

- **Chocolate** contains theobromine and caffeine, which stimulate the central nervous system and heart muscle, and relax smooth muscle tissue. This results in vomiting, diarrhea, rapid heart rate, seizures, and, in severe cases, death. Dogs that consume chocolate usually show symptoms after 2 - 4 hours.

- **Grapes and Raisins** can cause kidney failure in dogs. The first symptom is usually vomiting, which occurs within 24 hours after the dog eats them. Other symptoms of grape toxicity in dogs are lethargy, loss of appetite, diarrhea, and abdominal pain.

- **Onions and Garlic** as well as leeks and chives have sulfur-containing aromatic chemicals that can damage a dog's red blood cells and cause anemia, leading to weakness, lethargy, and digestive issues. Symptoms might occur within a day of eating these vegetables. However, they may only appear after several days, depending on how much the dog has eaten. Just 5g of onion or garlic can cause significant problems in a small dog.

- **Xylitol** is a sugar substitute found in many sugar-free products, such as chocolate, sugar-free gum, baked goods, cookies, and bread. It stimulates the release of insulin, causing a rapid drop in blood sugar levels at very low doses. The signs of hypoglycemia in dogs are lethargy, poor balance, collapse, and seizures, which can occur within 30 minutes to an hour after eating a product containing xylitol.

  The sugar substitute can also lead to liver failure in dogs. Signs that your dog is developing liver problems include jaundice, vomiting, and bleeding issues, such as small bruises on the skin and intestinal hemorrhages.

- **Avocado** contains a chemical called persin, which is toxic to dogs and can lead to vomiting, diarrhea, and other digestive issues.

- **Alcohol**, even in small amounts can cause alcohol poisoning in dogs. The signs that your dog has consumed alcohol occur within an hour of ingesting it and include symptoms like vomiting, diarrhea, coordination issues, and in severe cases, coma and respiratory failure.

- **Caffeine** is found in coffee, tea, energy drinks, chocolate, and some medications and is rapidly absorbed into the bloodstream of dogs. It is a central nervous system stimulant that can lead to restlessness, rapid heart rate, tremors, seizures, and, in severe cases, death.

- **Macadamia Nuts** can cause muscle weakness, tremors, vomiting, poor coordination, abdominal pain, stiffness, lameness, and elevated body temperature 12 hours after a dog has consumed them.

- **Fruits with pits.** The pits and seeds of fruits like peaches, cherries, apricots, and plums contain cyanide compounds, which can be poisonous if ingested. The poison reduces the body's ability to use oxygen, resulting in difficulty breathing, abdominal pain, confusion, diarrhea, lethargy, trembling, and a swollen abdomen.

- **Fatty Foods** such as fatty meats, hot dogs, bacon, butter, and fried foods can cause pancreatitis in dogs, a painful inflammation of the pancreas. The condition causes the pancreas to make enzymes that damage the dog's intestines. The most common signs of pancreatitis include vomiting, diarrhea, abdominal pain, reduced appetite, and lethargy.

- **Bones** don't generally cause poisoning in dogs. However, they are dangerous for your dog. Cooked bones, especially those from chicken and other poultry, can splinter and cause blockages, tears, or punctures in a dog's digestive system.

- **Dairy** contains a type of sugar called lactose which requires the enzyme, lactase to digest it. Many dogs lack this enzyme and are, therefore, lactose intolerant. When these dogs consume dairy products like milk or cheese they may suffer digestive upset, including abdominal pain and diarrhea.

- **Salt** can cause a condition called salt toxicosis in dogs. If they eat too much salty food the level of sodium in the blood increases resulting in water being drawn out of the cells into the bloodstream to rebalance the electrolytes. It can damage the cells and affect the brain and nervous system.

- **Harmful Spices and Seasonings**. In large quantities, herbs and spices including garlic, nutmeg, salt, black pepper, and chives can be harmful to dogs.

Preventing Accidental Ingestion of Toxic Foods for Dogs

Dogs generally aren't too fussy about what they eat and are keen to try anything they can get their paws on. Your furry friend is a bit like a toddler. Leave them unsupervised and they are bound to get up to mischief.

Considering the number of human foods that are toxic to dogs, you must treat these foods with caution and ensure that they are stored out of your dog's reach. These are some suggestions for managing your dog's food environment:

Secure Storage

All toxic foods and beverages must be securely stored in containers with tight-fitting lids.

Elevated Surfaces

Keep toxic food and beverages out of reach of your dog. They should be locked away in cupboards or kept on elevated surfaces such as shelves that your dog can't reach.

Garden and Yard Safety

Many toxic foods, such as avocados, macadamia nuts, fruit with pits, grapes, and herbs could be growing in your garden. In addition, there are many plants that contain poisonous chemicals that can make your pet sick. Tulips, lilies, oleander, and philodendrons, to name a few, should be avoided, especially if your dog tends to chew on the plants.

Be Mindful of Visitors

If your dog loves your friends and family and looks at them with puppy dog eyes whenever they have food, it's best to ask them not to feed your dog. They may not be familiar with the foods that can harm your dog. It's better to be safe than sorry.

Training your Dog

Apart from ensuring that you don't give your dog toxic foods and storing them out of reach, the best way to secure your dog's nutritional safety is to train them to only eat foods in their dish or given to them by you.

Basic Commands

Sit, down, and stay, are the 3 most basic commands every dog should know. You can use these commands to teach your dog to sit and wait for his food rather than jumping up and digging in before their dish has touched the floor.

Encourage Positive Responses With Positive Reinforcement

It's pleasing to people when others notice the good things they have done or achieved. Your four-legged friend is no different. Dogs also respond well to positive reinforcement for behaving as you would like them to instead of being punished for bad behavior. So, at feeding time, reward your dog for sitting and waiting for his meal rather than punishing them for jumping up to get it.

Ensuring Your Dog Isn't Protective of Their Food

Dogs can be protective of what they perceive to be theirs. In the case of food, they may not let anyone or another dog near them when they are eating or chewing on a favorite treat. Teach them that you are in charge, even of their food, so that if they manage to get hold of a toxic food, you can safely take it away from them.

Enrolling in Instructional Courses or Training Classes

Puppies are encouraged to attend socialization classes to learn how to behave around people and other dogs. You can enroll in more formal training classes for guidance on how to teach your dog to obey basic commands so that they can live in harmony with you.

CHAPTER 5
COOKING METHODS AND TECHNIQUES

The cooking method you choose when cooking your dinner depends on the desired outcome. If you want a crunchy outer coating on your chicken drumstick, you will probably fry it. If you're cooking spaghetti, you will boil it, and if you are making a cake, you will bake it in the oven.

Not only does your chosen cooking method decide the texture and flavor of your meal, but it also affects the nutritional value. With that in mind, how you cook your best friend's meals is an important consideration for how you are going to meet their nutritional requirements and for making meals that suit their personal food preferences.

Cooking for Optimal Nutrition

The last thing you want to do after buying the best quality ingredients you can afford for your homemade dog food is ruin the nutrient content. The purpose of making your dog's meals from scratch using fresh wholesome ingredients is to promote her/his health and wellbeing.

Some people will tell you that the best choice for your dog is a raw food diet, others will insist dogs should only eat traditional dog food in the form of kibble, while others suggest the only way to go is grain-free. As we have already discussed, there are pros and cons for each type of canine nutrition.

This chapter is dedicated to the benefits of wholesome homemade dog food and how to cook it to get the most out of it and keep your dog drooling for more, their tail wagging, and their coat shining.

Raw Feeding Considerations

Many consider a raw food diet to be closest to a dog's ancestral eating habits. Wolves, for example, are hunters feeding predominantly on raw meat, bones, and the organs of the animals they kill. They are also known to eat various fruits including apples, pears, cherries, berries, and melon.

People who feed their dogs a raw diet report benefits, such as improved coat condition, better energy levels, and improved dental health. However, these claims have not been proven by scientific studies.

If you believe this is the diet of choice for your dog, you must consider several important factors. Firstly, consult with your veterinarian to ensure it's a suitable choice for your pet, and that it will meet their specific dietary needs.

Secondly, balanced nutrition is most important. Raw diets should consist of a variety of meats, bones, organs, and vegetables to ensure your dog receives all essential nutrients. Food-safety guidelines for handling and storing raw meat products must be followed to prevent food-borne illnesses in your dog and your family.

Finally, monitor your dog's health and digestion closely when transitioning to a raw diet and adjust as necessary.

Raw vs. Cooked (Pros and Cons)

The table below details the pros and cons of raw food and cooked food diets to help you decide whether raw or cooked food is best for your pet.

	Raw Food Diet	Cooked Homemade Food
Pros	• Control over quality and source of ingredients. • Management of food allergies and intolerances. • Management of inflammatory bowel disease. • Benefits lacking scientific evidence include improved digestibility and stool consistency, better dental health, and enhanced skin and coat condition.	• Control over quality and source of ingredients. • Tailored meals to meet your pet's nutritional requirements and preferences. • Management of food allergies and intolerances.
Cons	• May result in an imbalance in calcium and phosphorus. • Lack of variety may cause nutrient deficiencies. • High risk of food-borne diseases. • Splintered bones can be a choking hazard and can cause intestinal blockages. • High-quality raw ingredients can be expensive.	• The diet may not be nutritionally balanced. • Requires knowledge of the complex nutritional requirements for canine diets. • Risk of overfeeding, resulting in weight gain. • Time consuming. • Expensive.

Balancing Nutrient Loss and Safety

Food safety is as critical for your four-legged friend as it is for you. Considering how dogs seem to love rooting around in the garbage and eating anything they find from spoiled food to dead rats, you may think their health isn't affected by bacteria, fungi, and viruses found in such items.

While they may choose their tasty morsels quite indiscriminately, they are still prone to stomach troubles and food-borne diseases. To avoid such problems and to keep your dog in tip-top shape, it is recommended to feed them cooked meals instead of taking a chance on the safety of raw ingredients.

When the food is heated, pathogens such as bacteria are destroyed, reducing the risk of illness. One of the biggest concerns about cooking food is the loss of nutrients when heat is applied to food. Along with the changes in color, texture, taste, and aroma that occur when food is cooked, micronutrients may also be lost.

Some vitamins are destroyed by heat and others are drawn out of the food, especially when cooked in large amounts of water. Levels of vitamin C and the B-group of vitamins are substantially reduced by high temperatures and cooking food in boiling water. Fat-soluble vitamins A, D, E, and K leach out of food when they are cooked in fat such as frying. However, they are more heat stable than the water-soluble vitamins.

Minerals can also leach out of foods when they are boiled. Levels of magnesium, potassium, sodium, and calcium in your dog's food are reduced when food is soaked in water or boiled in large amounts of water.

Fortunately, by choosing the best cooking method for the type of food you're cooking, you can retain most of the nutritional value while ensuring food safety and the health of your best friend.

Cooking Methods

To cook food, heat is applied in various forms. It may be wet or dry, direct or indirect, or very hot or more temperate. You may use a variety of cooking techniques when cooking meals for yourself and your human family. They include steaming, boiling, frying, roasting, grilling, broiling, and baking, each of which uses a different source of heat.

The same cooking methods can be used to prepare your dog's homemade meals. Since each technique offers pros and cons for nutrition, flavor and texture, try to use a variety of different cooking methods when cooking for your dog to tempt their nose and taste buds.

Boiling: Retaining

Boiling is a method of cooking that involves cooking meat, vegetables, and starchy foods in large amounts of water at roughly 100°C (212°F). The high temperature destroys some of the vitamin C and B-group vitamins. In addition, the same vitamins along with some of the minerals in the food leach out into the water. However, the fat-soluble vitamins in the food are more stable and are retained in the food.

Not all is lost when boiling your pet's food. The nutrient-rich water can be used to cook rice or added to the meals to make nutritious gravy, retaining most of the nutritional value of the raw ingredients.

Boiling is the ideal cooking method for dogs with oral issues who struggle to chew harder, tougher food. It helps to soften the ingredients, making it easier for them to eat.

Baking: Enhancing Flavor

Baking food in the oven is a cooking technique that uses dry heat. The carbohydrates, sugars, fats, and proteins undergo chemical changes on the surface of the meat or vegetables to create a pleasing brown color, and a sweeter, caramelized flavor.

Although the food is cooked at high temperatures, most of the nutritional value is maintained. Small losses of vitamin C and B-group vitamins occur due to their heat instability, but levels of minerals and fat-soluble vitamins remain close to the original value of the raw ingredients.

Slow Cooking: Tenderizing Ingredients

Cooking meat in a slow cooker at lower temperatures for a longer time is a great way to tenderize tough cuts of meat. It helps to soften the connective tissues, making the meat easy to eat, even for dogs that have problems with their teeth.

The water used in the cooking process can be incorporated into tasty, meaty gravy to retain any of the nutrients that leach into it and add flavor to your dog's meal.

Pan-Frying: Moderate Use

Frying food in fat brings about similar changes to the surface of the food as baking. Unfortunately, although it is a quick way to cook food, the oil or other fat used in the cooking process is problematic.

Firstly, you may lose some of the fat-soluble vitamins as they leach into the fat. Secondly, it increases the fat content of home-made dog food. A high fat diet may result in a higher calorie intake than your dog needs, causing weight gain. Too much fat in a dog's diet has also been linked with the development of pancreatitis (Cridge et al., 2022).

Occasionally frying your pet's food is okay but try to keep this cooking method for special occasions or when you are pushed for time.

Steaming: Preserving Nutrients

Steaming is the best way to preserve the nutrients in food. The food is cooked by surrounding it by steam rather than boiling it water, which is often discarded. Even the heat sensitive vitamins are retained at levels close to the original content in the raw ingredients.

Balancing Cooking Techniques

Think about your own typical meal. You probably use a combination of cooking techniques to make your plate of food more visually, texturally, and aromatically appealing. For example, you may serve a grilled steak with fried potatoes, and steamed vegetables.

Your dog also benefits from a variety of cooking methods when you prepare their homemade food. Try to combine cooking methods to maximize nutritional value and to enhance the flavors and textures of the ingredients.

CHAPTER 6
MEAL PLANNING
AND PREPARATION

As a health-conscious person, you probably spend a fair amount of time thinking about what you're going to eat every day to support your wellbeing and maintain a healthy weight. You naturally know when you need to eat and how much food you need to feel satisfied. You eat balanced meals that include foods from all the food groups and are familiar with how to adapt your diet to increase your intake of nutrients or reduce your calories.

Your dog's diet doesn't demand the same amount of attention when they eat traditional dog food in the form of kibble. Someone else has done all the necessary calculations for you and formulated a food to meet your dog's nutritional requirements. However, if you choose to prepare homemade meals, you must spend just as much time planning their meals, shopping for the best ingredients, and preparing tasty dishes as you do for your own diet.

Without the proper planning and time-efficient preparation, adding an extra cooking schedule to your daily routine can quickly become overwhelming, especially when life gets busy. Use the templates, examples, and tips in this chapter to keep on top of your pet's dietary requirements so that it doesn't become a chore, and your dog continues to benefit from lovingly prepared wholesome meals.

Weekly Meal Plans

Millions of dogs around the world thrive on eating the same kibble diet every single day. It may be nutritionally balanced and fill their bellies, but have you considered that dogs might enjoy some variety? Think about how excited they get when there's a chance they may be offered a tasty morsel off your plate.

Unlike humans, dogs are satisfied eating the same dish for several meals in a row. That means, your meal planning is simplified, and you only have to prepare 2 - 3 different dishes every week. For example, you could alternate between chicken, beef, and chickpeas mixed with a variety of grains and dog-friendly vegetables and herbs for added flavor and nutrients.

The recipes included in this homemade dog food guide have been created to tempt your pet's taste buds. Use them, along with the handy meal plan calculation template below to create a healthy menu for your pooch that is nutritionally balanced and has them begging for more.

Dog's Meal Plan Calculation Template

Use this template to make planning your furry friend's meals easier. Once you know how much energy and the percentage of macronutrients they require, you can translate your calculations into actual food.

Homemade Dog Food Meal Planning Template

Dog's weight in kg:
RER Calculation: RER = (Dog's weight in kg)^{¾}x 70   = _____kCal per day
MER Calculation: MER = RER x Activity factor (Refer to the table in chapter 1)   = _____kCal per day   (Alternatively, refer to the table of average energy requirements according to weight in chapter 1.)

Macronutrients	Percentage of MER: (Use percentages most appropriate for your dog. Refer to chapter 1)	Grams per Day:	Units of Food
Protein Requirements: 8.8 - 30%	____% of MER = _____kCal	_____kCal ÷ 4 = _____g	(30g lean meat = 1 food unit = 7g of protein and 3g of fat) Units of protein: =___g protein ÷ 7 =_____units
Fat Requirements: 12.4 - 60% (Note: Too much fat can cause pancreatitis)	____% of MER = _____kCal	_____kCal ÷ 9 = _____g	Fat from meat (3g per unit): = ___units of protein x 3g of fat = ____g of fat from meat*
Carbohydrates Requirements: 10 - 78.8%	____% of MER = _____kCal	_____kCal ÷ 4 = _____g	(1 food unit = 15g of carbohydrates) Units of carbohydrates: = _____g CHO ÷ 15g =_____units of CHO** food

Portions per Meal/Snack:	Breakfast:	Dinner:	Snacks/Treats:
Protein	__units = ___g of meat	__units = ___g of meat	__units = ___g of meat
Fat	__units = ___g of fat from oil***	__units = ___g of fat from oil***	__units = ___g of fat from oil***
Carbohydrate:			
· Grains	__units = ___g	__units = ___g	__units = ___g
· Starchy vegetables	__units = ___g	__units = ___g	__units = ___g
· Non-starchy vegetables	__units = ___g	__units = ___g	__units = ___g
· Fruit	__units = ___g	__units = ___g	__units = ___g

*If your dog needs more fat than is provided by the meat, subtract the total provided by protein foods from the total grams of fat calculated in the previous column, and divide the difference by 5 to get the number of teaspoons of oil you can add to the food (1 unit of fat = 5g).This is usually only necessary for very active dogs with high energy requirements.

**CHO = Carbohydrate

***Only add oil if your dog needs extra fat in their diet

Dog Food Unit Lists

When a Registered Dietitian creates a diet plan for you, they use a system of food exchanges to make it simpler to plan meals (*Healthy Eating, Food Exchange Lists*, n.d.). The foods are grouped together based on the amount of protein, fat, and carbohydrate they contain, giving you the following groups:

· Proteins

· Fats

· Starches

- Fruits

- Vegetables - starchy and non-starchy

- Dairy products

You can use a similar system to simplify planning your dog's menu. However, since many dogs are lactose intolerant, the dairy group is left out. Use the table below as a guide for determining your furry friend's portion sizes. The portion sizes suggested in the table are the equivalent of 1 unit of food. For example, 30g of lean beef is 1 unit of protein.

Homemade Dog Food Units

Lean Protein: 1 unit = 7g of protein and 3g of fat	
30g / 1oz chicken - skin removed 30g / 1oz turkey - skin removed 30g / 1oz lean beef 30g / 1oz pork - trimmed of excess fat 30g / 1 oz fish such as salmon, tuna, cod	30g / 1 oz lamb - trimmed of excess fat 1 egg ½ cup / 115g / 4oz legumes such as lentils, chickpeas, soybeans (**Note on legumes**: This protein unit doubles as a unit of carbohydrates)
Carbohydrates: 1 unit = 15g of carbohydrate	
⅓ cup / 60g / 2oz cooked rice (white/brown) ⅓ cup / 60g / 2oz cooked barley	½ cup / 120g / 4.2oz cooked oatmeal ⅓ cup / 60g / 2oz cooked quinoa

Starchy Vegetables: 1 unit = 15g of carbohydrate	
½ cup / 75g / 2.6oz cooked sweet potato ½ cup /80g / 2.8oz corn ½ cup / 65g / 2.3oz green peas (fresh) ½ cup / 65g / 2.3oz cooked parsnips ½ cup / 75g / 2.6oz cooked sweet potato	½ cup /90g / 3oz cooked beetroot ½ cup / 120g / 4.2oz cooked pumpkin ½ cup /110g/ 3.8oz cooked butter-nut squash
Non-Starchy Vegetables: 1 unit = 5g of carbohydrate	
½ cup / 65g / 2.3oz cooked carrots ½ cup / 70g / 2.5oz cucumber ½ cup / 65g / 2.3oz celery ½ cup / 60g / 2oz green beans	Serve the following vegetables in moderation to avoid digestive issues: ½ cup / 35g / 1.2oz broccoli, cauli-flower, cabbage, spinach
Fruit: 1 unit = 15g of carbohydrate	
½ cup /80g / 2.8oz berries - blue-berries, cranberries, raspberries, strawberries ½ cup / 60g / 2oz apples ½ cup / 75g / 2.6oz bananas ½ cup / 80g / 2.8oz melon/cantaloupe ½ cup / 80g / 2.8oz mango	½ cup / 60g / 2oz oranges ½ cup / 80g / 2.8oz peaches - pit removed ½ cup / 55g / 1.9oz pears ½ cup / 80g / 2.8oz pineapple ½ cup / 75g / 2.6oz watermelon

Measurement Conversion Chart

Wherever possible, the ingredients in the recipes are listed as household measures, grams, ounces, milliliters, and fluid ounces. If you are using your own recipes, here's a handy measurement conversion chart.

Weight		Volume		
Grams*	Ounces	Household Measure	Milliliters*	Fluid Ounces
30	1	1 Teaspoon	5	⅙
60	2	1 Tablespoon	15	½
85	3	2 Tablespoons	30	1
110	4	¼ Cup	60	2
140	5	⅓ Cup	70	3
170	6	½ Cup	120	4
200	7	⅔ Cup	160	5
225	8	¾ Cup	180	6
255	9	1 Cup	240	8

*Metric measures (grams and milliliters) have been rounded off

Let's put it all together and look at some sample meal plans for small, medium, and large-sized dogs using the meal plan calculation template.

Sample Meal Plan for a Senior Small Breed Dog

Examples of small breed dogs (<5.5 - 10 kg):

· Yorkshire Terrier

· Maltese Poodle

· Chihuahua

· Pug

· Dachshund

· Corgi

- French Bull Dog

- Pekingese

- Miniature Schnauzer

- Papillon

Skippy is a 12-year-old neutered Yorkshire Terrier that weighs 6.6 lb. and goes for a slow, short walk once a day.

Dog's weight in kg: 3 kg

RER Calculation:
RER = (Dog's weight in kg) ^{¾} x 70
= $(3kg)^{¾}$ x 70
=160 kCal per day

MER Calculation:
MER = RER x Activity factor (Refer to the table in chapter 1)
= 160 x 1.4 (senior dog activity factor)
= 224 kCal per day

(Alternatively, refer to the table of average energy requirements according to weight in chapter 1.)

Macronutrients	Percentage of MER: (Use percentages most appropriate for your dog. Refer to chapter 1)	Grams per Day:	Units of Food
Protein Requirements: 8.8 - 30%	30% of MER = 30% of 224 kCal = 67 kCal	kCal of protein 4 67 ÷ 4 = 16.8g	(30g lean meat = 1 food unit = 7g of protein and 3g of fat) Units of protein: = 16.8g protein ÷ 7 = 2.4 units of lean meat

Fat	40% of MER	kCal of fat 9	Fat from meat (3g per unit):
Requirements: 12.4 - 60%	= 40% of 224 kCal	90 ÷ 9	= 2.4 units of protein x 3g of fat
(Note: Too much fat can cause pancreatitis)	= 90 kCal	= 10g	= 7.2g fat from meat*
			Note: Skippy is an old dog who is not very active, therefore no extra fat is added to his food.
Carbohydrates	30% of MER	kCal of CHO ÷ 4	(1 food unit = 15g of carbohydrates)
Requirements: 10 - 78.8%	= 30% of 224 kCal	67 ÷ 4	Units of carbohydrates:
	= 67 kCal	= 16.8g	= 16.8g CHO ÷ 15g
			= 1.12 units of CHO** food
Portions per Meal/Snack:	Breakfast:	Dinner:	Snacks/Treats:
Protein	1.2 units = 36g of meat	1.2 units = 36g of meat	0 units = 0g of meat
Fat	0g of fat from oil***	0g of fat from oil***	0g of fat from oil***
Carbohydrate:			
· Grains	⅓ unit = 20g rice	⅓ unit = 20g rice	0 units = 0g
· Starchy vegetables	⅙ unit = 20g pumpkin	⅙ unit = 20g pumpkin	0 units = 0g
· Non-starchy vegetables	0 units = 0g	0 units = 0g	0 units = 0g
· Fruit	0 units = 0g	0 units = 0g	⅕ unit = 12g apple

*If your dog needs more fat than is provided by the meat, subtract the total provided by protein foods from the total grams of fat calculated in the previous column, and divide the difference by 5 to get the number of teaspoons of oil you can add to the food (1 unit of fat = 5g).This is usually only necessary for very active dogs with high energy requirements.

**CHO = Carbohydrate

***Only add oil if your dog needs extra fat in their diet

Sample Meal Plan for an Active Medium-Sized Dog

Examples of medium-sized dogs (11 - 26 kg):

- Border Collie
- Labrador Retriever
- Cocker Spaniel
- Boxer
- German Shepherd
- Poodle
- Beagle
- Bull Terrier
- American Staffordshire Terrier
- Dalmatian

Abby is an active 4-year-old female Labrador Retriever working as a seeing-eye dog for a man who walks 5 km per day. She is full of energy and loves to play in her spare time. She weighs 55 lb.

Dog's weight in kg: 25 kg			

RER Calculation:

RER = (Dog's weight in kg) $^{3/4}$ x 70

$\quad$ = (25kg) $^{3/4}$ x 70

$\quad$ = 782 kCal per day

MER Calculation:

Note: Although Abby is an active working dog, the minimum activity factor for working dogs is used to calculate her calorie requirements. Since she is a Labrador Retriever, which is a breed that is prone to weight gain and obesity, her weight must be closely monitored by her veterinarian.

MER = RER x Activity factor (Refer to the table in chapter 1)

$\quad$ = 782 x 2

$\quad$ = 1560 kCal per day

(Alternatively, refer to the table of average energy requirements according to weight in chapter 1.)

Macronutrients	Percentage of MER: (Use percentages most appropriate for your dog. Refer to chapter 1)	Grams per Day:	Units of Food
Protein Requirements: 8.8 - 30%	20 % of MER 20% of 1560 = 312 kCal	kCal of protein 4 312 ÷ 4 = 78g	(30g lean meat = 1 food unit = 7g of protein and 3g of fat) Units of protein: = 78g protein ÷ 7 = 11 units

Fat	20 % of MER	kCal of fat 9	Fat from meat (3g per unit):
Requirements: 12.4 - 60% (Note: Too much fat can cause pancreatitis)	20% of 1560 = 312 kCal	312 ÷ 9 = 35g	= 11 units of protein x 3g of fat = 33g of fat from meat[*]
Carbohydrates Requirements: 10 - 78.8%	60 % of MER 60% of 1560 = 936 kCal	kCal of CHO ÷ 4 = 936 ÷ 4 = 234g	(1 food unit = 15g of carbohydrates) Units of carbohydrates: = 234 g CHO ÷ 15g = 15.6 units of CHO[**] food
Portions per Meal/Snack:	**Breakfast:**	**Dinner:**	**Snacks/Treats:**
Protein	5 units = 150g of meat	5 units = 150g of meat	1 unit = 30g of meat
Fat	0 units of fat from oil[***]	0 units of fat from oil[***]	0 units of fat from oil[***]
Carbohydrate:			
• Grains	4 units = 240g rice	4 units = 240g quinoa	0 units = 0g
• Starchy vegetables	3 units = 240g corn	3 units = 225g sweet potato	0 units = 0g
• Non-starchy vegetables	1.5 units = 50g broccoli	1.5 units = 100g carrots	0 units = 0g
• Fruit	0 units = 0g	0 units = 0g	⅓ unit = 50g watermelon

*If your dog needs more fat than is provided by the meat, subtract the total provided by protein foods from the total grams of fat calculated in the previous column, and divide the difference by 5 to get the number of teaspoons of oil you can add to the food

(1 unit of fat = 5g).This is usually only necessary for very active dogs with high energy requirements.

**CHO = Carbohydrate

***Only add oil if your dog needs extra fat in their diet

Sample Meal Plan for Sedentary Large Breed Dog

Examples of large breed dogs (26 - 45 kg):

- Bullmastiff

- Great Dane

- Saint Bernard

- Great Pyrenees

- Newfoundland

- Irish Wolfhound

- Bernese Mountain Dog

- Anatolian Shepherd

- Alaskan Malamute

- Rottweiler

Enzo is a lovable, goofy Great Dane. Although he is only 5 years old, he has hip dysplasia making exercise painful for him. He has been neutered and he weighs 143 lb.

Dog's weight in kg: 65 kg
RER Calculation:
RER = (Dog's weight in kg)$^{3/4}$ x 70
= $(65)^{3/4}$ x 70
= 1600 kCal per day

MER Calculation:

Note: Enzo is a large-sized dog with hip dysplasia. He is not an active dog. As a Great Dane, he is also prone to thyroid disease which can result in weight gain. Therefore, the activity factor used to calculate Enzo's energy requirements is 1.2.

MER = RER x Activity factor (Refer to the table in chapter 1)

$\quad$ = 1600 x 1.2

$\quad$ = 1920 kCal per day

(Alternatively, refer to the table of average energy requirements according to weight in chapter 1.)

Macronutrients	Percentage of MER: (Use percentages most appropriate for your dog. Refer to chapter 1)	Grams per Day:	Units of Food
Protein Requirements: 8.8 - 30%	25% of MER 25% of 1920 = 480 kCal	kCal of protein 4 = 480 ÷ 4 = 120g	(30g lean meat = 1 food unit = 7g of protein and 3g of fat) Units of protein: = 120g protein ÷ 7 = 17 units
Fat Requirements: 12.4 - 60% (Note: Too much fat can cause pancreatitis)	25% of MER 25% of 1920 = 480 kCal	kCal of fat 9 = 480 ÷ 9 = 53g	Fat from meat (3g per unit): = 17 units of protein x 3g of fat = 51g of fat from meat

Carbohydrates	50% of MER	kCal of CHO 4	(1 food unit = 15g of carbohydrates)
Requirements: 10 - 78.8%	50% of 1920	= 960 ÷ 4	
	= 960 kCal	= 240g	Units of carbohydrates:
			= 240g CHO ÷ 15g
			= 16 units of CHO** food
Portions per Meal/Snack:	**Breakfast:**	**Dinner:**	**Snacks/Treats:**
Protein	8 units = 240g of meat	7 units = 220 g of meat	2 units = 60g of meat
Fat	0g of fat from oil***	0g of fat from oil***	0g of fat from oil***
Carbohydrate:			
• Grains	4 units = 240g barley	4 units = 240 g quinoa	0 units = 0g
• Starchy vegetables	2 units = 240g pumpkin	2 units = 150g sweet potato	0 units = 0g
• Non-starchy vegetables	3 units = 100g spinach	3 units = 195g carrots	0 units = 0g
• Fruit	0 units = 0g	0 units = 0g	2 units = 60g apple & 80g melon

*If your dog needs more fat than is provided by the meat, subtract the total provided by protein foods from the total grams of fat calculated in the previous column, and divide the difference by 5 to get the number of teaspoons of oil you can add to the food (1 unit of fat = 5g).This is usually only necessary for very active dogs with high energy requirements.

**CHO = Carbohydrate

***Only add oil if your dog needs extra fat in their diet

Batch Cooking Tips

The great thing about preparing your own dog food is that you can cook large batches and store them in the fridge or freezer until you need them. Although your four-legged companions enjoys a bit of variety in their diet, they are happy to eat the same meal twice a day, every day.

Here are some handy tips for cooking large quantities of homemade dog food:

1. Create your dog's meal plan and menu.

2. Choose your recipe or recipes. You may want to begin with 1 or 2 recipes.

3. Make a shopping list and buy all the ingredients you need.

4. Ensure that you have enough single portion-sized containers in which to store the food.

5. To make preparation quicker and easier, use pre-prepared ingredients such as frozen vegetables such as peas, corn, and green beans.

6. If you're making a vegan dish, soak raw legumes in water overnight before cooking them.

7. Use a variety of cooking methods to enhance the flavor and nutritional value of your dog's meals. However, if you are pressed for time, you can simply cook everything together in the same large pot.

8. Once cooked, mix all the food together and allow the mixture to cool before portioning it into clean single portion-sized containers.

9. Cover with a tight-fitting lid and label the meal with the recipe name and the date it was prepared.

10. Store in the fridge or freezer until needed.

Freezing and Storage Guidelines

Your pet's fresh food must be stored in the same way you store your own food to avoid spoiling and the risk of food-borne illnesses. Use the tips below to maintain the quality of your large batches of homemade dog food.

- If you are making only enough food to feed your dog for 2 - 3 days, you can store it in a large glass or plastic container with an airtight lid in the fridge.

- When freezing your homemade dog food, it is preferable to dish it up into single portion containers. They save space in the freezer and allow you to remove only as much food as you need.

- Lids must be airtight to avoid spoiling.

- Label the meals with the name of the recipe and the date it was prepared.

- Use a first-in-first-out system to avoid keeping meals for an extended period of time, especially if it is being stored in the fridge.

- Prepared food can be stored in the fridge for 2 - 3 days and for 2 - 3 months in the freezer.

- Thaw frozen portions at room temperature or overnight in the fridge.

CHAPTER 7
TRANSITIONING TO HOMEMADE DOG FOOD

You've done your research and have decided to switch your best friend to a fresh food diet. For you, the benefits outweigh the drawbacks, so you've waded through the slightly complicated calorie requirement calculations, planned your pooch's menu, and now you're ready to make the switch.

Just like you, though, it's best to make dietary changes slowly to give your dog's digestive system time to adapt to the new food. The macronutrient composition and ingredients used to make homemade meals is likely to be very different to the kibble formulation your dog has been eating up until now.

This chapter will guide you in how to successfully transition your wet-nosed friend from a traditional dog food diet to a tasty wholesome meal plan.

Consult a Veterinarian

Book an appointment with your dog's veterinarian before you head off to stock your pantry with all the fresh ingredients you need to start preparing fresh homemade dog food. Discuss your dietary plan with them and ask them to assess your dog's overall health.

Establish your dog's health baseline.

The first visit before changing diets is to help you establish a baseline for your pet's health and wellbeing. Discuss any known health conditions your dog has and whether there are any specific dietary requirements for managing them. Also talk about their activity level and how you plan to adapt your homemade meals to ensure your friend's tail keeps wagging and their nutritional needs are being met.

Monitoring

Then, as you transition your dog to a homemade dog food diet, you can compare their health status at each subsequent vet's consultation to their baseline status. This will help you keep track of their condition and identify signs that may suggest the new diet may need to be adjusted.

It is generally recommended that you take your dog for a checkup once a year. However, it may be beneficial to visit the vet for more frequent check-ups when transitioning from traditional dog food to homemade dog food to ensure that health issues due to dietary imbalances can be identified before they become a problem. Aim for every 3 to 4 months for the first year you feed your dog homemade food, and weigh them every month.

Regular veterinary check-ups

A thorough checkup at the vet includes the following (da Costa et al., 2022):

- The vet will listen to your dog's heart and lungs to make sure there is no underlying heart disease or breathing problems.

- Palpating the abdomen can give the vet clues about the health of your dog's internal organs and pick up any swelling or abnormal lumps or masses. It also helps the vet identify if your dog is experiencing pain and the source of the pain.

- Your pet's eyes will be examined to look for diseases in the eye and to identify signs of illness elsewhere in the body.

- The ears will be examined for signs of bacterial infection, ear mites, polyps, and wax buildup.

- A dog's food plays an important role in maintaining oral health. Their teeth and gums will be checked during the consultation with the vet to look for signs of gum disease and tooth decay and damage.

- The veterinarian will check your dog's weight. A change in diet may cause your dog to gain or lose weight.

- The general condition of your dog's coat is affected by their diet as well as health problems. A dull, dry, and brittle coat, for example, may mean your pup needs more protein or fat in their diet.

Choose the Right Homemade Dog Food Recipes

How many times have you been disappointed by the results of a recipe you found online? Perhaps it was lacking flavor, or it didn't cook in the specified time, or you found there were gaps in the preparation instructions. You might have eaten it, but you wouldn't have prepared it again.

Internet recipes for homemade dog food can be just as problematic as the recipe you found for a social media influencer's grandma's chocolate chip cookies. Similarly, not all online sources of information can be trusted to have your furry friend's best interests at heart.

Because canine nutrition is complex, it is crucial to select only recipes you know you can trust to be nutritionally balanced. Those designed or approved by a veterinary nutritionist are the best. They encourage you to use quality ingredients and give you clear cooking instructions. Remember, the cooking method can also affect the nutritional value of your dog's meals.

A study on how well pet-parents adhere to guidelines and recipes designed for their dogs found that even though the majority reported not making any changes to the recipes they use to prepare their furry friend's meals, only 13% of the study participants were still using the same recipe a year after they switched to homemade dog food (Johnson et al., 2015). This had an impact on the nutritional value of their pet's meals.

The recipes included in part 2 have been carefully designed according to scientific recommendations to meet your pet's nutritional requirements. As such, it is recommended that you don't make any changes to the recipes, including ingredients, cooking methods, and storage instructions.

Gradually Transition Your Dog to a Fresh Food Diet

Whether you are simply changing to a different brand of commercial dog food or if you are transitioning them to a fresh homemade food diet, it is best to make gradual changes to your dog's diet. Doing so, gives their digestive system time to adapt and time for you to observe any adverse reactions to the new food (Staff 2022, American Kennel Club).

Commercial dog food has been formulated to meet your dog's nutritional needs and to be easy for your dog to digest. A sudden switch in the type of food your pet eats may disrupt digestion and cause gastrointestinal upset including vomiting, diarrhea, and loss of appetite.

The best way for you to monitor your dog's gut health is to keep an eye on their poop. There are bound to be some changes due to the different ingredients in your homemade meals, but if you are concerned about the frequency, volume, or change in texture, color, or odor, you should consult with your dog's veterinarian to help you identify the possible cause.

Another common adverse reaction to a new diet is symptoms of food allergy or intolerance. While gut problems are common signs that your pet's food is disagreeing with them, they may also become itchy and start scratching a lot, their skin may become inflamed and rashes may appear, or they may start losing their hair. A slow transition to a homemade diet allows you to identify potential problems with ingredients before they become a threat to your dog's health and wellbeing.

Be Flexible and Adjust Your Dog's Meal Plan

Establishing a healthy whole food meal plan for your dog takes time and there are likely to be stumbling blocks along the way. For example, you may discover that your pooch has an adverse reaction to some of the nutritious ingredients you have carefully selected to ensure that their meals provide all the energy and nutrients their body requires to be healthy.

You may also find that your dog becomes a picky eater and won't eat meals that contain pumpkin, they eat around the broccoli, or they absolutely refuse to eat the nutrient-rich liver you took time to prepare for them.

Whatever the case, if you are committed to feeding your dog a nutrient-dense whole food diet, you will need to be flexible and willing to adapt their plan to their changing needs due to illness, life stage, or disability, as well as their food preferences (Callon et al., 2017).

4-Week Transition Plan

Most vets advise people to take about a week to transition your dog from one type of diet to another to avoid adverse reactions (Liao et al., 2023). Taking your time to prepare a nutritious meal plan, slowly introduce the new food, and monitor your pet's tolerance of the change in diet, helps to ensure that the transition is smooth.

Use this 4-week transition to homemade dog food plan to successfully change your dog's diet without negatively affecting their health.

Week 1: Preparation

The first week is for laying the groundwork for your furry companion's new healthy diet. It includes the following steps:

1. Consult with your dog's veterinarian to discuss the proposed changes to your dog's diet, get advice about ensuring the diet is balanced, and establish your dog's baseline health to be

used as a reference to determine whether the new diet needs to be adapted to avoid any serious health issues.

2. Calculate your dog's calorie and macronutrient requirements.

3. Create a meal plan.

4. Choose the recipes you want to include in the meal plan, avoiding any known allergens or dislikes.

5. Shop for the ingredients and prepare the first batch of wholesome meals.

Week 2: Introduction to Total Transition

When you're ready to start introducing the new meals to your dog, remember to do it slowly, increasing the amount of homemade food every second day (Staff 2022, American Kennel Club). Use the following schedule to gradually transition your dog to fresh meals:

1. On days 1 and 2, replace a quarter of your dog's meals with the new homemade dog food. Monitor them for any signs of an adverse reaction.

2. On days 3 and 4, you can increase the amount of homemade food to half of your dog's meals. Continue to monitor for adverse effects.

3. On days 5 and 6, increase the amount of fresh food to three quarters of your dog's meals. Continue to monitor for adverse effects.

4. On the 7th day, assuming there haven't been adverse reactions to previous meals, your dog's meals can be 100% homemade food.

Week 3: Adjust and Fine-Tune the Meal Plan

By week 3, your dog should be enjoying the carefully calculated, lovingly prepared meals you have cooked for them. However, you may need to make some adjustments to the meal plan and your choice of recipes. Some of the common reasons you will need to adapt your dog's new meals include the following:

- Adverse reactions to the food such as vomiting, diarrhea, or itching.

- Your dog may not find the first recipes palatable, making it necessary to adapt the recipes by swapping the ingredients your dog doesn't enjoy with ingredients that have a similar nutrient profile.

- You may need to give your dog more or less food depending on whether they still seem to be hungry after their meals or doesn't finish the food in their dish.

If you have to make changes to your first homemade meals, follow the steps from week 2 to introduce the revised meals. If your dog had an adverse reaction to the food, it is advisable to return to their original diet for a few days until they no longer show any signs of gastrointestinal or other problems.

Be patient and persevere. Just because the first attempt wasn't as successful as you'd hoped, it doesn't mean a homemade food diet is not suitable for your dog. Often, it is a single ingredient that causes the problem, and by avoiding it, your dog will thrive on their new diet.

Week 4: Full Transition and Monitoring

The final stage is to monitor your dog's health as they continue to enjoy their tasty homemade meals. Weighing your dog and keeping an eye on their poop are the easiest ways for you to keep track of their health on your own.

Consult with the veterinarian every 3 to 4 months after changing your dog's diet to ensure your careful dietary planning is indeed meeting your pet's nutritional needs, and are not showing any signs of nutritional deficiencies.

CHAPTER 8
DOS AND DON'TS OF HOMEMADE DOG FOOD

You are almost ready to start cooking mouthwatering meals for your dog. Before you pick your recipes, here is a summary of everything you have learned about planning, preparing, and introducing your dog to homemade dog food.

8 Things You Must Do

#1 Research and Plan Thoroughly

If your furry companion is a purebred canine, research the features of the breed. Find out how tall they usually grow, whether they tend to gain weight, and what types of health conditions may affect them.

For crossbreeds, such as a Labrador Retriever cross Border Collie, research both breeds and ask your vet to help you examine your dog to figure out the most prominent characteristics of your dog.

Dogs that are a cross between several different breeds must be examined by their veterinarian. That said, you can still work out their nutritional needs by using their weight and general form.

Then, use the information you have learned to plan your dog's diet by calculating their calorie and macronutrient needs, and carefully selecting ingredients to create meals with high canine nutritional value that your dog will love.

Before you start cooking, plan how you will store the homemade dog food, and purchase the containers you will need. Ensure that their lids fit snugly and that you have enough space in your fridge or freezer to store them until you need them.

#2 Consult a Veterinarian

Book a consultation with your pet's veterinarian to discuss their overall health and wellbeing. Inform them of your intention to change your dog's food to a homemade dog food diet, and discuss the pros and cons, any health conditions that may affect your food choices, and the plan for monitoring their health during and after the transition.

#3 Prioritize Balanced Nutrition

It is equally crucial for a dog's diet to be nutritionally balanced. Dietary deficiencies can cause health issues for dogs. Therefore, you must be mindful of the nutrient value of the ingredients you choose when preparing homemade dog food.

Pay particular attention to the protein content of the diet, ensuring that your pet's meals contain all 10 of the essential amino acids. Also include foods, such as chia seeds and oily fish that contain essential fatty acids, and a variety of fruits, vegetables, and grains to meet their vitamin and mineral requirements (Feuer, 2006).

#4 Use Quality Ingredients

Buy the best quality ingredients you can afford when preparing homemade dog food. Focus on fresh whole foods, such as whole grains, dog-friendly vegetables, safe fruits, and unprocessed meat including lean beef, chicken, and fish.

Fresh and frozen pre-prepared vegetables can reduce the time you spend in the kitchen and can be included in your pet's meals. However, it's best to avoid processed foods that contain added salt, fat, preservatives, additives, and fillers.

#5 Include Variety

It is said that 'variety is the spice of life'. For homemade dog food, a wide range of different meals not only tempts your furry friend's taste buds but helps ensure that you provide your dog with all the nutrients they need to be healthy and thrive. Since each ingredient you choose contains different levels of macro and micronutrients, variety is the key to balanced nutrition.

#6 Maintain Portion Control

An overweight dog is susceptible to similar health conditions as an overweight person. Overfeeding your dog results in weight gain which places pressure on their joints and may result in chronic diseases, such as heart disease, hypertension, and diabetes. Too much of a good thing, even wholesome homemade dog food can be bad.

It is, therefore, crucial to give your dog only as much food as they need to support life and maintain a healthy weight. The easiest way to see if your dog is eating too much is to monitor their weight. If they start gaining weight, you may need to cut back on their portions.

#7 Gradually Transition

A sudden change in food can cause several problems for your dog. Gastrointestinal issues are the most common adverse reactions to a new diet. Dogs may feel nauseous or experience vomiting and diarrhea if you simply swap their old diet for the new homemade dog food.

Use the 4-week plan to transition your dog safely and successfully to their new feeding regime.

#8 Practice Food Safety

Your pooch may enjoy the disgusting morsels they find and eat when you're not watching. However, dogs are just as prone to food-borne illnesses as you are. For that reason, you must take the same precautions when preparing their food as you do when making yours.

Buy the freshest ingredients you can and store them safely at the correct temperature until you cook them. Once cooked, portion the meals into containers with airtight lids, allow them to cool and then store them in the fridge or freezer until you need them. Cooked foods can be kept in the fridge for 2 - 3 days and in the freezer for 2 - 3 months.

8 Things to Avoid Doing

#1 Don't Rely on a Single Recipe

It may be tempting to prepare the same recipe over and over again. After all, if your dog is eating it, it must taste okay. However, even though dogs that are fed traditional dry dog food eat the same thing for every meal, your homemade meals must include some variety to ensure you are providing your dog with the wide range of nutrients they require to keep their body structure and function in tip-top shape.

Remember, commercial dog foods are specifically formulated to meet a dog's energy, protein, fat, vitamin, and mineral requirements. The same level of nutrition in homemade dog food can only be achieved by including a wide range of dog-friendly ingredients because each one provides different amounts and types of nutrients.

#2 Don't Overdo Seasonings and Spices

Dogs have a more sensitive sense of smell and taste than humans do. Consequently, food that tastes bland to you is full of delicious flavor for your pooch. Their meals don't need a lot of seasonings and spices for them to enjoy their food.

It's also critical to remember that some seasonings and spices can be toxic to dogs. Onions and garlic, for example, can cause anemia, and a high intake of salt can cause high levels of sodium in the blood, resulting in water being drawn out of the dog's cells and a condition called salt toxicosis that affects the brain and nervous system.

#3 Don't Include Harmful Ingredients

Apart from the toxic seasonings and spices, there are several other foods that may harm your dog. The artificial sweetener, xylitol, is particularly toxic, as are grapes, raisins, chocolate, and macadamia nuts. Refer to the list in chapter 4 if you need a reminder of the foods not to include in your homemade dog food.

#4 Don't Neglect Essential Nutrients

Some nutrients can be synthesized by your dog's body, but most must be supplied by the diet. Those that must be included in your homemade dog food include the 10 essential amino acids, unsaturated fatty acids, vitamins, such as vitamin A, vitamin E, vitamin D, and vitamin B1, and minerals including calcium, phosphorus, magnesium, potassium, and sodium.

Nutrient deficiencies can result in poor health. Therefore, your veterinarian may suggest adding a nutritional supplement to your dog's homemade meals.

#5 Don't Overcomplicate Meals

Keep it simple. Your dog isn't looking for gourmet meals. Their food may be one of the highlights of their days, but they will be equally as excited with chicken, rice, and some carrots as they would be if you cooked them a 3-course meal.

Instead, save yourself time in the kitchen by focusing on the nutritional value of the meals and preparing several different recipes to keep in the freezer that you can rotate to keep mealtimes interesting and full of essential nutrients.

#6 Don't Assume All Human Foods are Safe

Do your research before including human foods in your dog's diet. An ingredient that is good for you and adds your favorite flavors to your meals isn't necessarily good for your dog.

A list of foods to avoid has been included in chapter 4. It's a good place to start, but if the food you wish to include in your furry friend's food is not included in any of the lists in this book, it is best to do your research on its safety for dogs before adding it to their meal plan. When in doubt, ask your veterinarian or veterinary nutritionist.

#7 Don't Ignore Allergies and Sensitivities

Food allergies can be mild or severe, depending on how your dog's immune system reacts to the offending food. A mild allergic reaction may cause a few irritating symptoms, such as excessive scratching or a bout of diarrhea, but an anaphylactic allergic reaction can cause difficulty breathing and swelling in the muzzle and skin. It usually requires immediate medical attention (Tizard, 2018).

#8 Don't Neglect Regular Vet Check-Ups

You can usually tell if there is something bothering your dog. They might be more lethargic than usual, they've might have gone off their food, or they might be vomiting persistently. However, some dogs keep going with a wag in their tail even when they feel sick.

Hence, you must be diligent about taking them for regular vet check-ups to identify any health issues before they become a problem. This is especially true when you make changes to their diet. An unbalanced homemade dog food meal plan could cause nutritional deficiencies that can have a negative impact on your dog's health and wellbeing.

Take your dog to the vet at least once a year for a routine checkup. It is advisable to increase the frequency for the first year when you transition your dog to homemade dog food.

Time to Start Cooking

Your research is done. You've learned about canine nutrition and the nutrients your dog needs in their diet, and you've figured out the calculations for calorie and macronutrient requirements.

You know which foods to include in your dog food recipes and which ones to avoid, and you are familiar with the taste, texture, and nutritional benefits and drawbacks of a variety of cooking methods.

Now, you can start putting the theory into practice with the selection of tasty, healthy, nutritionally balanced dog-friendly recipes in part 2. Everything is covered from treats and rewards to soups and gravies, from main meals with lean meat, chicken or fish to vegan dishes, and recipes to tempt dogs with special dietary requirements.

So, put on your apron, take out the pots, and start preparing the best meals your dog has ever eaten.

PART 2

CHAPTER 9
TREATS AND REWARDS

Nothing gets a dog's tail wagging as much as the promise of a tasty treat. As satisfying as it is to see the excitement in your furry friend's eyes when you take their favorite snack out of the jar, remember that the food you offer between meals contributes to their daily calorie intake. If you give them too many treats, they run the risk of gaining weight.

Most dogs are food-motivated and will do anything for a mouthwatering reward. Whether you want your dog to sit, stay, or roll over, or if you simply want to give them a treat, prepare a batch of some of the treats and rewards recipes. They are all wholesome snacks for your dog that can easily be included in their meal plan.

Recipe notes:

1. To ensure that your dog treats are nutritionally balanced and contribute to your dog's vitamin and mineral intake, you may want to add a nutritional supplement to the recipes. Ask your veterinarian for advice on supplements.

2. The nutritional value for each recipe is an estimate based on the recipe analysis (Recipe Calorie and Nutrition Calculator, n.d.). The exact values depend on the size of the treats, and, in some cases, the brand of ingredients used.

PEANUT BUTTER BANANA BITES

Ingredients

1 (115 gms/4oz) banana (ripe to overripe)

½ cup (125 gms/4.4oz) cup peanut butter (no sugar, sweetener, or salt added)

1 cup (90 gms/3oz) rolled oats

1 tablespoon ground flaxseeds (optional for added nutrition)

Instructions

1. Preheat the oven to 180°C (350°F).
2. In a mixing bowl, mash the banana until smooth.
3. Stir in the peanut butter until the mixture is well combined.
4. Gradually add the rolled oats and ground flaxseeds, mixing well until all ingredients are incorporated.
5. Line a baking sheet with parchment paper.
6. Turn out the banana mixture onto a floured surface and roll out until it's roughly ½ cm (¼ in) thick.
7. Using a cookie cutter, cut the mixture into shapes of your choice.
8. Transfer the cutouts to the prepared baking sheet.
9. Place in the oven and bake for 10-12 minutes, or until the edges are golden brown.
10. Remove from the oven and allow them to cool completely on a wire rack before treating your dog.

Nutrition Information: Makes 20 small biscuit treats.

Calories: 61 kCal

Carbohydrate: 5.3g

Protein: 2.6g

Fat: 3.5g

SWEET POTATO CHEWS

Ingredients

2 (500 gms/8oz) sweet potatoes

Instructions

1. Preheat the oven to 120°C (250°F).
2. Line 2 baking sheets with parchment paper.
3. Wash and scrub the sweet potatoes thoroughly. Pat them dry using a kitchen towel.
4. Cut the sweet potatoes into slices ½ cm (¼ in) thick. For large dogs, slice the sweet potatoes lengthways, and for smaller dogs, slice them into disks across the width of the sweet potatoes.
5. Place the sweet potato slices on the baking sheets, ensuring they do not overlap.
6. Bake for 2- 3 hours, turning halfway through the cooking time.
7. They are ready when they are dried out but still a bit chewy.
8. Allow them to cool completely. Store in an airtight container in the fridge for up to 3 weeks.

Nutrition Information: Makes 40 small / 20 large (depends on the size of the sweet potatoes)

Small:

Calories: 8 kCal Protein: 0.2g   Carbohydrate: 2g Fat: 0g

Large:

Calories: 16 kCal Protein: 0.4g   Carbohydrate: 4g Fat: 0g

CARROT CRUNCHIES

Ingredients

1 (115 gms / 4oz) banana (ripe to overripe)

6 - 8 (900 gms / 32oz) carrots (grated)

⅛ cup (30 ml / 1 fl oz) apple puree (unsweetened)

¼ cup (60 ml / 2 fl oz) orange juice (freshly squeezed)

1 ½ cups (180 gms / 6.3oz) flour

1 cup (90 gms / 3oz) rolled oats

Instructions

1. Preheat the oven to 180°C (350°F).
2. Mash the banana and add to a mixing bowl with the carrots and apple puree. Mix to combine.
3. Add the water and mix well to combine.
4. Stir in the flour and oats until well combined.
5. Tip the mixture onto a floured surface and knead until smooth.
6. Roll out the dough until it is ½ cm (¼ in) thick.
7. Use a cookie cutter to cut the dough into your shape of choice.
8. Line a baking sheet with parchment paper and place the cut-out cookies on the sheet.
9. Bake for 25 minutes or until browned. Remove the crunchies from the baking sheet and cool on a wire rack.
10. Cool completely before storing in an airtight container.

Nutrition Information: Makes 40 crunchies.

Calories: 34kCal

Carbohydrate: 7.2g

Protein: 0.9g

Fat: 0.2g

CHICKEN AND RICE BISCUITS

Ingredients

1 cup (170 gms/6oz) chicken meat (cooked)

½ cup (100 gms/3 ½ oz) rice (cooked)

½ cup (120 ml / 4 fl oz) chicken stock (salt-free)

1 large egg

4 ½ cups (680 gms/24oz) flour

Instructions

1. Preheat oven to 180°C (350°F).
2. Line a large baking sheet with parchment paper.
3. Add the chicken meat, rice, and chicken stock to a food processor and blend until smooth.
4. Transfer the chicken mixture to a large mixing bowl.
5. Lightly beat the egg and add it to the chicken mixture. Add 4 cups of the flour and mix until well combined to make a stiff dough. Add the remaining flour if your mixture is too wet.
6. Turn the dough out onto a floured surface and knead until smooth.
7. Roll it out until it is about 1cm (½ in) thick.
8. Use a cookie cutter of your chosen shape to cut the rolled-out dough into biscuits and place them on the lined baking sheet.
9. Place them in the oven and bake for 25 - 30 minutes or until browned.
10. Cool completely on a wire rack.
11. Store in an airtight container in the fridge for 3- 4 days. (The biscuits can be stored in the freezer for longer.)

Nutrition Information: Makes 50 small biscuits.

Calories: 63kCal

Protein: 2.7g

Carbohydrate: 12g

Fat: 0.3g

BEEFY MEATBALLS

Ingredients

450 gms (1 lb.) lean ground beef

1 egg

½ cup (40 gms / 1.3 oz) carrots (finely grated)

½ cup (90 gms / 3.1 oz) zucchini (finely grated)

¼ cup (30 gms / 1 oz) flour

Instructions

1. Preheat your oven to 180°C (350°F).
2. In a large mixing bowl, combine the lean ground beef, egg, finely grated carrots, and zucchini. Mix thoroughly until all the ingredients are well incorporated.
3. Gradually sprinkle the flour over the meat mixture, continuing to mix until the flour is evenly distributed throughout.
4. Shape the mixture into small meatballs, using your hands. Aim for consistent sizes to ensure even cooking.
5. Line a baking sheet with parchment paper or lightly grease it to prevent sticking.
6. Place the meatballs on the prepared baking sheet, ensuring there's space between each one for even cooking.
7. Bake in the preheated oven for about 20-25 minutes, or until the meatballs are fully cooked and browned on the outside.
8. Once cooked, remove the meatballs from the oven and let them cool for a few minutes.

Nutrition Information: Makes 20 meatballs.

Calories: 52kCal

Protein: 7.3g

Carbohydrate: 1.5g

Fat: 1.6g

PUMPKIN TREATS

Ingredients

2 ½ cups (300 gms / 10.6 oz) whole wheat flour

2 eggs

½ cup (240 gms / 8.5 oz) cooked pumpkin (mashed)

2 Tbsp (30 gms / 1 oz) peanut butter (unsweetened)

Instructions

1. Preheat your oven to 175°C (350°F).

2. In a large mixing bowl, whisk the eggs until lightly beaten.

3. Add the mashed cooked pumpkin and peanut butter to the bowl. Mix thoroughly until all the ingredients are well combined.

4. Gradually add the whole wheat flour, mixing continuously until a dough forms. The dough should be firm but pliable. If it's too sticky, you can add a bit more flour.

5. On a floured surface, roll out the dough to about ½ cm (¼ in) thick.

6. Using a cookie cutter or knife, cut the dough into your desired shapes or simply create small disks.

7. Line a baking sheet with parchment paper or lightly grease it to prevent sticking.

8. Place the cut-out treats on the prepared baking sheet, leaving a bit of space between each one.

9. Bake in the preheated oven for about 20-25 minutes, or until the treats are golden brown and firm to the touch.

10. Remove from the oven and let the treats cool completely on a wire rack.

11. Once cooled, store the treats in an airtight container for up to a week.

Nutrition Information: Makes 25 treats.

Calories: 59kCal

Carbohydrate: 10.2g

Protein: 2.1g

Fat: 1.1g

TURKEY AND SWEET POTATO BITES

Ingredients

2 cups (160 gms / 5.6 oz) rolled oats
½ cup (140 gms / 5 oz) cooked sweet potatoes (mashed)
¾ cup (180 ml / 6 fl oz) water
1 egg
2 cups (170 gms / 6 oz) cooked turkey (shredded)

Instructions

1. Begin by preheating your oven to 180°C (350°F).
2. In a large mixing bowl, combine the rolled oats, mashed sweet potatoes, and shredded turkey.
3. Beat the egg in a separate bowl and then fold it into the mixture.
4. Gradually add the water, mixing continuously until the ingredients bind together to form a cohesive dough.
5. On a lightly floured surface, take small portions of the dough and shape them into bite-sized balls or patties. If the mixture is too sticky, you can add a bit more oats.
6. Arrange the bites on a baking sheet lined with parchment paper, ensuring they're spaced out to allow for even cooking.
7. Place in the oven and bake for 20-25 minutes, or until the bites are golden brown and firm.
8. Remove from the oven and allow the turkey and sweet potato bites to cool completely on a wire rack.
9. Once cooled, store in an airtight container in the refrigerator for up to a week.

Nutrition Information: Makes 36 biscuits.

Calories: 36 kCal

Carbohydrate: 4.6g

Protein: 2.6g

Fat: 0.8g

DUCK JERKY STRIPS

Ingredients

450 gms (1 lb.) duck breasts

Instructions

1. Begin by placing the duck breasts in the freezer for about 1-2 hours. This will make slicing them more manageable.

2. Preheat your oven to its lowest setting, typically around 65°C-90°C (150°F-200°F).

3. Remove the duck breasts from the freezer and use a sharp knife to slice them into thin strips, approximately ⅛ inch thick. If possible, slice against the grain, as this will make the jerky more tender for your dog.

4. Pat each strip dry with paper towels to remove any excess moisture.

5. Arrange the duck strips on a baking sheet lined with parchment paper or on a wire rack placed over a baking sheet. Ensure the strips are evenly spaced and not touching each other.

6. Place the baking sheet in the oven and bake for 2-4 hours. The exact baking time will depend on the thickness of the slices and your oven's specific temperature. You're aiming for the duck to be dried out but still slightly chewy.

7. Check the duck strips periodically to ensure they don't become overly dry or crispy.

8. Once done, remove the jerky strips from the oven and let them cool completely on a wire rack.

9. Store the duck jerky strips in an airtight container in the refrigerator for up to 2 weeks.

Nutrition Information: Makes roughly 20 jerky strips.

Calories: 29 kCal

Carbohydrate: 0g

Protein: 5g

Fat: 0.9g

LAMB AND MINT TREATS

Ingredients

1 cup (130 gms / 4.6 oz) cooked lamb (shredded)

2 tsp mint (finely chopped)

2 ½ cups (300 gms / 10.6 oz) whole wheat flour

1 cup (250 ml / 8.4 fl oz) plain low-fat yogurt

Instructions

1. Preheat the oven to 180°C (350°F).
2. In a large mixing bowl, combine the shredded lamb and finely chopped mint.
3. Add the plain low-fat yogurt to the lamb and mint mixture and mix well until all the ingredients are well combined.
4. Gradually fold in the whole wheat flour, continuously mixing until a firm dough forms. If the mixture seems too dry, you can add a splash of water; if too wet, add a bit more flour.
5. Once the dough is ready, place it on a floured surface and roll it out to about ½ cm (¼ in) thick.
6. Using a cookie cutter of your choice, cut shapes from the dough. Alternatively, you can shape them into small disks using your hands.
7. Line a baking sheet with parchment paper and arrange the treats on it, ensuring they don't touch each other.
8. Bake in the preheated oven for 20-25 minutes, or until the treats turn golden brown and are firm to the touch.
9. Once baked, remove the treats from the oven and let them cool completely on a wire rack.
10. Store the cooled treats in an airtight container for up to a week.

Nutrition Information: Makes 10 treats.

Calories: 56kCal

Carbohydrate: 4g

Protein: 6.4g

Fat: 1.3g

SWEET POTATO TREATS

Ingredients

1 (250 gms/4 oz) sweet potato (peeled and diced)

2 ½ cups (300 gms/10.6 oz) whole wheat flour

2 large eggs

¼ cup (60 ml/2 fl oz) plain low-fat yogurt

Instructions

1. Preheat the oven to 180°C (350°F).
2. In a pot with boiling water, cook the diced sweet potato until they are tender, about 10-12 minutes. Drain the water and let the sweet potatoes cool for a few minutes.
3. Mash the cooked sweet potatoes in a large mixing bowl until smooth, and without any lumps.
4. Add the whole wheat flour to the mashed sweet potatoes and mix well.
5. Incorporate the eggs and plain low-fat yogurt into the mixture, stirring until a dough forms. The dough should be firm but pliable.
6. Roll out the dough on a floured surface until it's about ½ cm (¼ in) thick.
7. Use cookie cutters to cut shapes from the dough or shape them into small disks with your hands.
8. Line a baking sheet with parchment paper and arrange the treats on it, making sure they are spaced apart.
9. Bake in the preheated oven for 30-40 minutes, or until the treats are golden brown and firm to the touch.
10. Allow the treats to cool on a wire rack completely before storing or serving.
11. Once cooled, store the treats in an airtight container for up to a week.

Nutrition Information: Makes 32 treats.

Calories: 47kCal

Carbohydrate: 8.9g

Protein: 1.6g

Fat: 0.4g

CHEESE AND BACON TREATS

Ingredients

4 strips (100 gms/3.5 oz) back bacon (trimmed of fat, diced, and cooked until crispy)

½ cup (60 gms/2 oz) Swiss cheese (shredded)

1 ½ cups (120 g/4.2 oz) rolled oats

2 large eggs

Flour for kneading and rolling.

Instructions

1. Preheat the oven to 180°C (350°F).

2. In a large mixing bowl, combine the cooked and diced back bacon with the shredded Swiss cheese.

3. Add the rolled oats to the mixture, stirring to incorporate evenly.

4. Beat the eggs in a separate bowl and then add them to the mixture. Mix until all ingredients are combined and form a dough. If the dough is too sticky, gradually add a bit of flour until it reaches the desired consistency.

5. Sprinkle some flour onto a clean surface, and turn out the dough onto it. Knead the dough a few times until smooth, adding more flour if necessary to prevent sticking.

6. Roll out the dough to about ½ cm (¼ in) thick.

7. Use cookie cutters to cut desired shapes from the dough, or shape them into small disks or bone shapes with your hands.

8. Line a baking sheet with parchment paper and arrange the treats on it, making sure they don't touch each other.

9. Bake in the preheated oven for 20-25 minutes, or until the treats turn golden brown and are firm to the touch.

10. Allow the treats to cool on a wire rack completely before storing or serving.

11. Once cooled, store in an airtight container for up to a week.

Nutrition Information: Makes 30 treats.

Calories: 48kCal

Protein: 3.2g

Carbohydrate: 4.3g

Fat: 2g

SALMON AND PEA COOKIES

Ingredients

1 cup (140 gms/4.9 oz) salmon fillet

2 cups (500 ml/16.9 fl oz) water

1 cup (160 gms/5.6 oz) fresh or frozen peas (cooked and mashed)

3 cups (360 gms/13.7 oz) whole wheat flour

Instructions

1. Preheat the oven to 180°C (350°F).

2. In a medium-sized pot, add the salmon fillet and water. Bring to a boil and then let it simmer for about 10-15 minutes or until the salmon is fully cooked.

3. Once cooked, remove the salmon from the water and let it cool. Reserve thewater.

4. After cooling, flake the salmon into small pieces, ensuring there are no bones.

5. In a large mixing bowl, combine the flaked salmon and mashed peas.

6. Gradually add the whole wheat flour to the mixture. As you're adding the flour, add the reserved salmon water, a little at a time, to help combine the ingredients and form a dough. You may not need all the water; just add enough to achieve a firm but pliable dough consistency.

7. Turn out the dough onto a floured surface and knead for a few minutes until smooth.

8. Roll the dough to about ½ cm (¼ in) thick.

9. Using cookie cutters, cut your desired shapes from the dough. Alternatively, shapethemintosmalldiscswithyourhands.

10. Line a baking sheet with parchment paper and arrange the cookies on it, ensuring they are spaced apart.

11. Bake in the preheated oven for 25-30 minutes or until the cookies are golden brown and firm to the touch.

12. Allow the cookies to cool on a wire rack completely before storing or serving.

13. Once cooled, store the cookies in an airtight container for up to a week.

Nutrition Information: Makes 30 cookies.

Calories: 54 kCal

Carbohydrate: 9.9g

Protein: 2.4g

Fat: 0.4g

PORK AND APPLE MEATBALLS

Ingredients

450 gms (1 lb.) lean ground pork

1 apple (peeled and grated)

1 ½ cups (45 gms /1.6 oz) baby spinach – finely chopped

1 Tbsp (15 ml/0.5 fl oz) flaxseed oil

1 Tbsp fresh parsley (chopped)

Instructions

1. Preheat the oven to 180°C (350°F).
2. In a large mixing bowl, combine the lean ground pork and grated apple.
3. Finely chop the baby spinach and add it to the pork and apple mixture.
4. Add the flaxseed oil and chopped fresh parsley to the mixture. Mix everything well until all ingredients are evenly distributed.
5. Using your hands, shape the mixture into small meatballs, approximately the size of a golf ball or smaller depending on your dog's size.
6. Place the formed meatballs on a baking sheet lined with parchment paper or lightly greased.
7. Bake in the preheated oven for 20-25 minutes, or until the meatballs are fully cooked and lightly browned on the outside.
8. Remove from the oven and allow the meatballs to cool on a wire rack.
9. Once cooled, store in an airtight container in the refrigerator for up to 5 days.
10. Serve the meatballs as a treat or food topper, ensuring they are an appropriate size for your dog.

Nutrition Information: Makes 20 meatballs.

Calories: 65kCal

Carbohydrate: 1.9g

Protein: 4.1g

Fat: 4.6g

SARDINE CRUNCHIES

Ingredients

90 gms (3oz) sardines (canned in spring water)

60 gms rolled oats

Flour for kneading and rolling.

Instructions

1. Preheat the oven to 180°C (350°F).
2. Drain the sardines and place them in a mixing bowl. Mash them up using a fork until they're broken down into smaller pieces.
3. Add the rolled oats to the mashed sardines and mix until combined. The mixture should be sticky and slightly wet.
4. If the mixture feels too wet, you can add a bit of flour to help bind it. If it's too dry, add a tiny amount of water.
5. Sprinkle some flour onto a clean surface and turn out the sardine mixture onto it. Knead gently until the mixture becomes more dough-like.
6. Roll the dough to about ½ cm (¼ in) thick.
7. Use a cookie cutter to cut shapes or simply slice it into small squares using a knife.
8. Place the shapes on a baking sheet lined with parchment paper, ensuring they're spaced apart.
9. Bake in the preheated oven for 12-15 minutes or until the crunchies are golden brown and firm to the touch.
10. Remove from the oven and allow them to cool on a wire rack.
11. Once cooled, store in an airtight container for up to a week.

Nutrition Information: Makes 10 crunchies.

Calories: 41 kCal

Protein: 3g

Carbohydrate: 4.1g

Fat: 1.4g

TURKEY BACON TWISTS

Ingredients

1 package (280 gms/10 oz) turkey bacon

Instructions

1. Preheat the oven to 180°C (350°F).
2. Take a piece of turkey bacon from the pack. If it's too wide, you can cut it lengthwise to get 2 thinner strips.
3. Take one strip (or 2 if they're thin) and twist them tightly into a spiral shape. If you're using 2 strips, you can twist them together, creating a braided appearance.
4. Place the twisted turkey bacon on a baking sheet lined with parchment paper.
5. Repeat the process for the rest of the turkey bacon strips.
6. Bake in the preheated oven for 10-12 minutes or until the twists are crispy and golden brown.
7. Remove from the oven and let them cool on a wire rack.
8. Once cooled, store in an airtight container for up to a week.

Nutrition Information: Makes 12 twists.

Calories: 20kCal

Carbohydrate: 0g

Protein: 3g

Fat: 0.5g

CHAPTER 10
SOUPS, BROTHS, STOCKS, AND GRAVIES

For people, soups, broths, stocks, and gravies are versatile additions to your meals. They can be a complete meal on their own, or used to make tasty, comforting stews, or poured over your meal to add extra flavor.

Many recipes for such flavor-packed delights include ingredients such as onion, garlic, and salt that are toxic to dogs. Therefore, as tempting as it may be to share your soup or gravy with your four-legged friend, it is advisable to make a separate pot for them that include only dog-friendly ingredients.

Cook up large batches of the recipes in this chapter and store them in the freezer. The soups can be a nutritious meal for your dog, especially if they have problems with their dental health. The broths and stocks can be used as the basis for other dishes, and the gravies can be added to cooked meat, vegetables, and grains to add nutrient-rich moisture to your dog's meals.

Recipe notes:

1. Soups, broths, stocks, and gravies may contain enough protein, carbohydrate, and fat to be a complete meal for your dog. However, in some cases the calorie or protein content is very low, and the fat content is very high, making the dish a tasty addition to a meal rather than a meal itself.

2. The nutritional value for each recipe is an estimate based on the recipe analysis (Recipe Calorie and Nutrition Calculator, n.d.). The exact values depend on the size of the portions, and, in some cases, the brand of ingredients used.

CHICKEN AND VEGETABLE BROTH

Ingredients

1 (60 gms / 2 oz) carrot (diced)

1 celery stalk, including the leaves (chopped)

½ cup (100 gms / 3.5 oz) green beans (sliced)

4 - 6 (500 gms / 1 lb.) chicken thighs (skin removed)

1.5 liters (3 pints) water

Instructions

1. Place the chicken thighs in a large pot.
2. Add the diced carrot, chopped celery, and sliced green beans to the pot.
3. Pour in the 1.5 liters (3 pints) of water, ensuring that the chicken and vegetables are fully submerged.
4. Bring the mixture to a boil over medium-high heat.
5. Once boiling, reduce the heat to low and let it simmer for 1-1.5 hours. This allows the flavors to meld and the broth to become rich in nutrients.
6. After simmering, remove the chicken thighs from the broth and set them aside to cool. Once cooled, debone the chicken thighs, discard the bones, and shred the meat.
7. Return the shredded chicken to the pot and stir to combine.
8. Let the broth cool down to room temperature.
9. Once cooled, you can serve a suitable portion to your dog. The broth can be given as a tasty hydrating treat or mixed with their regular food for added moisture and flavor.
10. Store the remaining broth in the refrigerator in an airtight container for up to 4 days. If you want to store it for a longer period, consider freezing it in portion-sized containers or ice cube trays for easy access.

Nutrition Information: Makes 6 cups.

Calories: 168kCal

Carbohydrate: 2.3g

Protein: 24.5g

Fat: 6.2g

BEEF AND RICE GRAVY

Ingredients

1 kg (2 lb.) beef bone marrow bones

2 (120 gms/4 oz) carrots (chopped)

2 celery stalks (chopped)

3 liters (6.3 pints) water

1 cup (180 gms/6.3 oz) rice (raw)

Instructions

1. In a large pot, place the beef bone marrow bones.

2. Add the chopped carrots and celery stalks to the pot.

3. Pour in the 3 liters (6.3 pints) of water, ensuring the bones and vegetables are fully submerged.

4. Bring the mixture to a boil over medium-high heat.

5. Once boiling, reduce the heat to low and let it simmer for about 2 hours. This will allow the marrow, collagen, and other nutrients from the bones to leach into the water, creating a rich broth.

6. After 2 hours, strain out the bones and vegetables, discarding them and keeping the liquid broth.

7. Return the broth to the pot and add the raw rice.

8. Cook the rice in the broth over medium heat until it becomes soft and breaks down, which should take about 20-25 minutes. Stir occasionally to prevent sticking. As the rice cooks and breaks down, it will thicken the broth, creating a gravy-like consistency.

9. Once the rice is fully cooked and the mixture has thickened to a gravy consistency, remove the pot from heat and allow it to cool to room temperature.

10. Store the remaining gravy in the refrigerator in an airtight container for up to 3 days. You can also freeze it in portion-sized containers for longer storage up to 2 – 3 months.

Nutrition Information: Makes 12 cups.

Calories: 112 kCal	Carbohydrate: 4.4g
Protein: 2g	Fat: 12g*

*Note the high fat content. Only serve small portions of this gravy to your dog.

PUMPKIN AND QUINOA SOUP

Ingredients

2 Tbsp (30 ml/1 fl oz) flaxseed oil

4 cups (120 gms/4 oz) pumpkin (diced)

½ tsp (2.5 ml/0.1 fl oz) ground cinnamon

4 cups (1 liter/2 pints) water

½ cup (125 ml/4.2 fl oz) plain low-fat yogurt

1 cup quinoa

Instructions

1. Heat the flaxseed oil in a large pot over medium heat.
2. Add the diced pumpkin to the pot and sauté for about 5-7 minutes, or until the pumpkin begins to soften.
3. Sprinkle in the ground cinnamon and stir well, allowing the cinnamon to toast slightly and release its aroma.
4. Add the water to the pot and bring the mixture to a boil.
5. Once boiling, reduce the heat to low and allow the pumpkin to simmer until it is completely soft, about 15-20 minutes.
6. While the pumpkin is simmering, rinse the quinoa under cold water until the water runs clear. This helps to remove any saponin that can give the quinoa a bitter taste.
7. Add the rinsed quinoa to the pot with the pumpkin and continue to simmer for an additional 15 minutes, or until the quinoa is fully cooked and has become translucent.
8. Once the quinoa is cooked and the pumpkin is soft, use an immersion blender or transfer the soup to a blender in batches to blend until smooth.
9. Return the blended soup to the pot and stir in the plain low-fat yogurt. This will give the soup a creamy texture and a slight tangy flavor.
10. Heat the soup over low heat just until it's warmed through. Do not let it boil after adding the yogurt, as this can cause it to curdle.

11. Once heated through, remove the pot from the heat and serve the soup warm or cold, but not hot. Store in the fridge in an airtight container for 2 - 3 days, or in the freezer for 2 - 3 months.

Nutrition Information: Makes 12 cups.

Calories: 128 kCal

Carbohydrate: 16g

Protein: 4.1g

Fat: 5.1g

FISH AND SPINACH STOCK

Ingredients

450 gms (1 lb.) fish bones

3 cups (750 ml / 1.5 pints) water

4 Tbsp (60 ml / 2 fl oz) fresh lemon juice

1 cup (30 gms / 1.1 oz) spinach (shredded)

Instructions

1. Start by rinsing the fish bones under cold water. This helps to remove any residual scales, blood, or impurities from the bones.

2. In a large pot, combine the rinsed fish bones, water, and fresh lemon juice.

3. Place the pot over medium heat and bring the mixture to a gentle simmer. As it heats up, skim off any foam or impurities that rise to the surface using a ladle or skimmer.

4. Once the mixture is simmering, reduce the heat to low and allow it to simmer gently for about 20-25 minutes.

5. After 20-25 minutes, add the shredded spinach to the pot. Stir gently to ensure the spinach is submerged in the stock.

6. Continue to simmer the mixture for an additional 10-15 minutes. This allows the flavors of the spinach to infuse into the stock.

7. After simmering, remove the pot from the heat and allow the stock to cool slightly.

8. Use a fine-mesh strainer to strain the stock, discarding the fish bones and spinach.

9. Transfer the strained stock to a clean container or jar and allow it to cool completely.Store in the fridge in an airtight container for 2 - 3 days, or in the freezer for 2 - 3 months.

Nutrition Information: Makes 4servings.

Calories: 13 kCal

Carbohydrate: 0.6g

Protein: 2.3g

Fat: 0.2g

CARROT AND CHICKEN GRAVY

Ingredients

450 gms(1 lb.) chicken fillets

½ cup (60 gms/2 oz) carrots (diced)

½ cup (80 gms/2.8 oz) frozen green peas

3 cups (750 ml/1.5 pints) water

2 Tbsp (10 gms/0.4 oz) corn flour

½ cup (125 ml/1/4 pint) water

Instructions

1. In a large pot, add the chicken and vegetables to 3 cups of water.

2. Bring the mixture to a boil over medium-high heat. Once boiling, reduce the heat to low and let it simmer for about 20-25 minutes, or until the chicken is fully cooked and the vegetables are tender.

3. After the chicken is cooked, remove the fillets from the pot and shred them into bite-sized pieces using 2 forks. Set the shredded chicken aside.

4. In a separate bowl, whisk together the corn flour and the ½ cup of water until smooth, ensuring there are no lumps. This mixture will serve as a thickening agent for the gravy.

5. Gradually pour the corn flour mixture into the pot, stirring continuously. This will ensure that the gravy thickens evenly without forming lumps.

6. Return the shredded chicken to the pot and stir to combine.

7. Allow the gravy to simmer for an additional 5-7 minutes, stirring occasionally, until it reaches your desired consistency.

8. Once the gravy is thickened to your liking, remove it from the heat.

9. Allow the gravy to cool to a safe temperature before serving. Store in the fridge in an airtight container for 2 - 3 days, or in the freezer for 2 - 3 months.

Nutrition Information: Makes 6 cups.

Calories: 96 kCal

Carbohydrate: 4.2g

Protein: 18.9g

Fat: 0.4g

POTATO AND BEEF STOCK

Ingredients

1 kg (2 lb.) beef bone marrow bones

1 large (280 gms / 9.8 oz) potato (peeled and diced)

2 celery stalks (chopped)

3 liters (6.3 pints) water

½ tsp (2.5 ml / 0.1 fl oz) dried rosemary

Instructions

1. Start by preparing the beef bone marrow bones. Ensure they are clean and free of any debris.

2. In a large pot or Dutch oven, combine the beef bone marrow bones, peeled and diced potato, chopped celery stalks, and dried rosemary.

3. Pour in the 3 liters of water to cover the ingredients.

4. Place the pot on medium-high heat and bring the mixture to a boil.

5. Once boiling, reduce the heat to low, cover the pot with a lid, and let it simmer for about 2-3 hours. This will allow the flavors to meld and the bone marrow to release its nutrients into the stock.

6. After the stock has simmered, strain it to remove any solid remnants, leaving you with a clear broth.

7. Allow the stock to cool to room temperature before serving it to your dog. Store in the fridge in an airtight container for 2 - 3 days or in the freezer for 2 - 3 months.

Nutrition Information: Makes 12 cups.

Calories: 112 kCal

Carbohydrate: 4.4g

Protein: 2g

Fat: 12g

**Note the high fat content. Only serve small portions of this stock to your dog.

LAMB AND RICE SOUP

Ingredients:

4 (1½ kg/3.3 lb.) lamb shanks (cooked)

3 liters (6.3 pints) water

¼ cup (80 ml/2.7 fl oz) apple cider vinegar

½ cup (100 gms/3.5 oz) green beans (chopped)

1 cup (180 gms/6.3 oz) rice (raw)

Instructions

1. Start by ensuring the lamb shanks are fully cooked and boneless. You can either cook them yourself or use leftover cooked lamb shanks.

2. In a large pot or Dutch oven, combine the cooked lamb shanks (boneless), water, and apple cider vinegar.

3. Place the pot on medium-high heat and bring the mixture to a boil.

4. Once boiling, reduce the heat to low, cover the pot with a lid, and let it simmer for about 15-20 minutes to infuse the flavors.

5. While the soup is simmering, rinse the raw rice thoroughly under cold water.

6. After the soup has simmered and developed flavor, add the rinsed raw rice and chopped green beans to the pot. Stir to combine all the ingredients.

7. Continue to simmer the soup on low heat for another 20-25 minutes or until the rice is fully cooked and the green beans are tender.

8. Remove the pot from the heat and allow the soup to cool to a safe temperature before serving it to your dog. Store in the fridge in an airtight container for 2 - 3 days, or in the freezer for 2 - 3 months.

Nutrition Information: Makes 16 cups.

Calories: 160kCal

Carbohydrate: 9.7g

Protein: 18.5g

Fat: 4.7g

Hearty Oat and Chicken Soup

Ingredients

1 kg (2 lb.) chicken thighs (skin and bones removed)

1 cup (90 gms / 3 oz) rolled oats

2 (120 gms / 4 oz) carrots (diced)

2 cups (400 gms / 14 oz) frozen green beans

1 cup (160 gms / 5.6 oz) frozen green peas

6 cups (1.5 liters / 3 pints) water

Instructions

1. Begin by removing the skin and bones from the chicken thighs, ensuring only the boneless and skinless meat is used.

2. In a large pot or Dutch oven, combine the boneless chicken thighs, diced carrots, and water.

3. Place the pot on medium-high heat and bring the mixture to a boil.

4. Once boiling, reduce the heat to low, cover the pot with a lid, and let it simmer for about 20-25 minutes or until the chicken is fully cooked and tender.

5. While the chicken is cooking, rinse the rolled oats under cold water to remove excess starch.

6. After the chicken is cooked, remove it from the pot and shred it into smaller, bite-sized pieces.

7. Return the shredded chicken to the pot and add the rinsed rolled oats, frozen green beans, and frozen green peas.

8. Stir well to combine all the ingredients, then cover the pot and let it simmer on low heat for an additional 10-15 minutes, or until the oats are fully cooked, and the vegetables are tender.

9. Remove the pot from the heat and allow the soup to cool to a safe temperature before serving it to your dog. Store in the fridge in an airtight container for 2 - 3 days or in the freezer for 2 - 3 months.

Nutrition Information: Makes 14 cups.

Calories: 179 kCal

Protein: 22.6g

Carbohydrate: 8.5g

Fat: 5.8g

PEA AND PORK GRAVY

Ingredients

1 cup (225 gms / ½ lb.) dried split peas

1 Tbsp (15 ml /o.5 fl oz) Canola oil

450 gms (1 lb.) ground pork

6 cups (1½ liters/3 pints) water

1 cup (120 gms/4 oz) carrots (diced)

¼ cup (45 gms/1.6 oz) red bell pepper (diced)

1 large (280 gms/9.8 oz) potato (peeled and diced)

½ tsp (2.5 ml/0.1 fl oz) ground cumin

Instructions

1. Begin by rinsing the dried split peas under cold water in a mesh strainer to remove any dirt or debris.

2. In a large pot or Dutch oven, heat the canola oil over medium heat.

3. Once the oil is hot, add the ground pork. Cook the pork, breaking it apart with a spatula, until it's browned and fully cooked.

4. To the pot, add the rinsed split peas, diced carrots, red bell pepper, potato, and the ground cumin. Stir to combine the ingredients.

5. Pour in the 6 cups of water and stir once more to ensure everything is well mixed.

6. Bring the mixture to a boil over high heat. Once boiling, reduce the heat to low, cover the pot, and allow the mixture to simmer for about 45-60 minutes. Check occasionally and stir to ensure nothing sticks to the bottom.

7. The gravy is done when the split peas are fully cooked and have broken down to thicken the gravy, and the vegetables are tender.

8. Remove the pot from the heat and allow the gravy to cool to a safe temperature before serving it to your dog. Store in the fridge in an airtight container for 2 - 3 days or in the freezer for 2 - 3 months.

Nutrition Information: Makes 12 cups.

Calories: 143 kCal

Protein: 14.4g

Carbohydrate: 15.3g

Fat: 2.7g

MIXED VEGETABLE STOCK

Ingredients

2 (120 gms/4 oz) carrots (diced)

4 stalks of celery (chopped)

1 large (225 gms/½ lb.) sweet potato (diced)

½ cup (90 gms/3.2 oz) red bell pepper (diced)

½ cup (50 gms/1.7 oz) cabbage (shredded)

8 cups (2 liters/4 pints) Water

Instructions:

1. Start by preparing all your vegetables: wash, peel where necessary, and dice or chop as indicated.

2. In a large stockpot or saucepan, combine the diced carrots, chopped celery, diced sweet potato, diced red bell pepper, and shredded cabbage.

3. Pour the 8 cups of water into the pot, ensuring that the vegetables are fully submerged.

4. Place the pot on the stove and turn the heat to high. Bring the mixture to a boil.

5. Once boiling, reduce the heat to low, allowing the stock to simmer gently.

6. Let the stock simmer for about 1 to 1½ hours, allowing the flavors of the vegetables to infuse into the water.

7. Periodically skim off any impurities or foam that may rise to the surface using a ladle or slotted spoon.

8. Once the stock has simmered and the flavors have melded, remove the pot from the heat.

9. Strain the stock through a fine-mesh sieve or cheesecloth into a large bowl or another pot, discarding the solids.

10. Allow the vegetable stock to cool before transferring it to storage containers. The stock can be stored in the refrigerator for up to a week or frozen for longer-term use. Use as a base for soups, stews, or any recipe requiring a vegetable stock.

Nutrition Information: Makes 8 cups of broth.

Calories: 11 kCal   Carbohydrate: 2g

Protein: <1g   Fat: 0g

Nutrition Information: Makes 10 cups thick vegetable soup.

Calories: 31 kCal   Carbohydrate: 7.1g

Protein: 0.8g   Fat: 0.1g

TUNA AND BROCCOLI BROTH

Ingredients

450 gms (1 lb.) fresh tuna (cut into large chunks)
½ (125 gms/4.4 oz) fennel (chopped)
2 celery stalks and leaves (finely chopped)
1 cup (165 gms/5.8 oz) broccoli (chopped)
6 cups (1½ liters/3 pints) water

Instructions

1. Place all the ingredients in a large pot.
2. Bring to the boil over high heat.
3. Reduce the heat and simmer gently for 20 to 30 minutes or until fish and the broccoli are cooked.
4. Stir to break up the fish and allow mixture to cool before serving to your dog.
5. Store in the fridge in an airtight container for 2 - 3 days or in the freezer for 2 - 3 months.

Nutrition Information: Makes 8 cups.

Calories: 117 kCal

Carbohydrate: 2.6g

Protein: 15.7g

Fat: 4.7g

CHAPTER 11
MAINS WITH MEAT

A hearty meaty bowl of food is bound to get your dog's mouth watering. Whether it's beef, lamb, chicken, or turkey, most dogs instinctively choose these high-protein foods (Roberts et al., 2017). Due to domestication, a dog's digestive system has adapted to an omnivorous diet, and carbohydrates, fruits, and vegetables have become an important part of their meal plan.

For that reason, the mains with meat recipes are a delicious combination of nutritious ingredients to ensure that your furry friend not only has a full belly after every meal, but their health and wellbeing are supported.

Recipe notes:

1. Ensure to regularly check in with your dog's veterinarian when transitioning them onto a homemade dog food diet. Since many human foods are toxic to dogs, it's not always possible to meet their nutrient requirements from food alone. Ask your vet for a recommendation for a nutrition supplement if your dog is showing signs of poor nutrition.

2. The nutritional value for each recipe is an estimate based on the recipe analysis (Recipe Calorie and Nutrition Calculator, n.d.). The exact values depend on the size of the portions and, in some cases, the brand of ingredients used.

CHICKEN AND BROWN RICE BOWL

Ingredients

2 Tbsp (30 ml / 1 fl oz) flaxseed oil

1.4 kg (3 lb.) ground chicken

4 cups (720 gms / 1.6 lb.) rice (raw)

2 ½ cups (375 gms / 0.8 lb.) frozen mixed vegetables (peas, corn, carrots, and green beans)

6 cups (1.5 liters / 3 pints) water

Instructions

1. In a large pot or Dutch oven, heat the flaxseed oil over medium heat.
2. Once the oil is warm, add the ground chicken. Cook, breaking the chicken apart with a spatula, until it's fully browned and cooked through.
3. Pour in the 6 cups of water and increase the heat to high. Bring the water to a boil.
4. Once boiling, add the raw rice to the pot, stirring to ensure it's evenly distributed.
5. Reduce the heat to low, cover the pot with a lid, and allow the rice to simmer for about 15-20 minutes.
6. After the rice has been cooking for 15-20 minutes, add the frozen mixed vegetables to the pot, stirring to combine.
7. Continue to cook the mixture on low heat for an additional 10-15 minutes or until the rice is fully cooked and the vegetables are tender.
8. Remove the pot from the heat and let the mixture cool down to a safe temperature before serving to your dog. Store in the fridge in an airtight container for 2 - 3 days or in the freezer for 2 - 3 months.

Nutrition Information: Makes 20 portions (±1 cup each).

Calories: 292 kCal

Protein: 23.8g

Carbohydrate: 31.5g

Fat: 6.9g

BEEF AND PUMPKIN STEW

Ingredients

1 Tbsp (15 ml /1 fl oz) Canola oil

450 gms (1 lb.) lean ground beef

250 gms (8.8oz) pumpkin (peeled and cubed)

1 (60 gms/2 oz) carrot (diced)

½ cup (80 gms/2.8 oz) frozen green peas

4 cups (1 liter/2 pints) water

Instructions

1. Start by heating the canola oil in a large pot or Dutch oven over medium-high heat.

2. Once the oil is hot, add the lean ground beef to the pot. Break the meat into smaller chunks using a spatula and cook until it's browned and fully cooked through.

3. Once the beef is browned, add the peeled and cubed pumpkin and the diced carrot to the pot. Stirtocombinewiththe beef.

4. Pour in the 4 cups of water, ensuring that the meat and vegetables are submerged. Bring themixtureto a boil.

5. Once boiling, reduce the heat to a simmer and let the stew cook for about 15-20 minutes or until the pumpkin and carrots are soft and easily pierced with a fork.

6. Add the frozen green peas to the pot, stirring them into the stew. Allow the stew to simmer for an additional 5 minutes, ensuring the peas are cooked through.

7. Remove the pot from heat and let the stew cool down to a safe temperature before serving to your dog. Store in the fridge in an airtight container for 2 - 3 days or in the freezer for 2 - 3 months.

Nutrition Information: Makes 8 portions (±1 cup each).

Calories: 142 kCal

Carbohydrate: 4.7g

Protein: 18g

Fat: 5.4g

TURKEY AND QUINOA DELIGHT

Ingredients

1 cup (200 gms/7 oz) quinoa, raw

4 cups (1 liter/2 pints) water

450 gms (1 lb.) ground turkey

1 ½ cups (225 gms/8 oz) frozen mixed vegetables (peas, corn, carrots, and green beans)

½ cup (75 gms/2.6 oz) blueberries

Instructions

1. Begin by rinsing the quinoa thoroughly under cold water using a fine-mesh strainer. This helps remove any bitter saponin from the quinoa's surface.

2. In a large pot, combine the rinsed quinoa and 4 cups of water. Bring the mixture to a boil over high heat. Once boiling, reduce the heat to low, cover the pot, and let the quinoa simmer for about 15 minutes or until the quinoa is soft and has absorbed all the water.

3. While the quinoa is cooking, in a separate large skillet or pan, cook the ground turkey over medium heat. Make sure to break the meat up into small crumbles and cook until fully browned and no pink remains.

4. Once the turkey is cooked, add the frozen mixed vegetables to the skillet. Stir and cook for about 5-7 minutes or until the vegetables are heated through and tender.

5. When the vegetables are cooked, fold in the blueberries, and stir gently to combine.

6. By now, the quinoa should be cooked. Fluff it with a fork and add it to the skillet with the turkey and vegetable mixture. Stir everything together, ensuring an even mix of all ingredients.

7. Remove the skillet from heat and allow the mixture to cool to room temperature before serving it to your dog. Store in the fridge in an airtight container for 2 - 3 days or in the freezer for 2 - 3 months.

Nutrition Information: Makes 8 portions (±1 cup each).

Calories: 229 kCal

Carbohydrate: 21.4g

Protein: 20.4g

Fat: 7.8g

GROUND BEEF AND NOODLES

Ingredients

1.4 kg (3 lb.) lean ground beef

1 package (500 gms / 1 lb.) macaroni

3 (180 gms / 6 oz) carrots (diced)

1 cup (30 gms / 1.1 oz) baby spinach (shredded)

Instructions

1. Start by preparing your ingredients. Dice the carrots and set them aside. Rinse the baby spinach and shred it finely.

2. In a large pot, boil water and cook the macaroni noodles according to the package instructions, ensuring they are well-cooked for easy digestion.

3. While the macaroni is boiling, in a separate pan, brown the lean ground beef over medium heat. Ensure that the beef is fully cooked, and break it up into small crumbles as it cooks.

4. Once the beef is browned, add the diced carrots to the pan and stir, letting them cook for about 5-7 minutes or until they're slightly softened.

5. After the carrots have softened, add the shredded baby spinach to the pan, and stir it into the beef and carrot mixture. Allow the spinach to wilt, which should take about 2-3 minutes.

6. Once the macaroni is cooked, drain the water and return the macaroni to the pot.

7. Combine the beef, carrot, and spinach mixture with the cooked macaroni in the pot. Stir well, ensuring everything is evenly mixed.

8. Let the mixture cool to room temperature before serving to your dog. Store in the fridge in an airtight container for 2 - 3 days or in the freezer for 2 - 3 months.

Nutrition Information: Makes 18 portions (±1 cup each).

Calories: 252k Cal

Carbohydrate: 21.8g

Protein: 27,4g

Fat: 5.3g

LAMB AND BARLEY CASSEROLE

Ingredients

1.4 kg (3 lb.) lean lamb (cubed)

1 kg (2 lb.) potatoes (cubed)

1 kg (2 lb.) carrots (sliced)

3 stalks of celery (chopped)

8 cups (2 liters/4.2 pints) water

500 gms (1 lb.) pearl barley, raw

Instructions

1. Begin by preparing your ingredients: Cube the lean lamb, ensuring there are no bones. Wash and cube the potatoes into bite-sized pieces. Wash, peel, and slice the carrots. Clean and chop the celery stalks.

2. In a large pot or Dutch oven, place the cubed lamb. Add the 8 cups of water, ensuring the meat is submerged. Bring to a boil over medium-high heat.

3. Once boiling, reduce the heat to low, letting the lamb simmer for about 30 minutes.

4. As the lamb is simmering, rinse the pearl barley in cold water using a sieve to remove any impurities.

5. After 30 minutes simmering the lamb, add the rinsed pearl barley to the pot.

6. Following the barley, add in the cubed potatoes, sliced carrots, and chopped celery. Stir well.

7. Simmer the mixture on low heat for another 40-45 minutes or until the barley is tender and fully cooked, and the lamb is soft. Make sure to stir occasionally to prevent any ingredients from sticking to the bottom of the pot.

8. Once everything is cooked thoroughly and the consistency is stew-like, remove the pot from the heat.

9. Allow the casserole to cool to room temperature before serving it to your dog. Store any leftovers in an airtight container in the refrigerator for up to 3 days. Ensure to reheat thoroughly before consuming.

Nutrition Information: Makes 24 portions (±1 cup each).

Calories: 228kCal

Carbohydrate: 26.9g

Protein: 19.5g

Fat: 4.6g

CHICKEN AND SPINACH MEDLEY

Ingredients

1½ cups (300 gms / 10.6 oz) brown rice, raw

1 cup (200 gms / 7 oz) green beans, fresh or frozen (chopped)

3 cups (900 gms / 2 lb.) meat from a rotisserie chicken (skin and bones removed)

1 cup (160 gms / 5.6 oz) mango (diced)

4 cups (120 gms / 4.4 oz) baby spinach (shredded)

Instructions

1. Begin by washing the brown rice under cold water using a fine-mesh sieve to remove excess starch so that the rice doesn't turn out too sticky when cooked.

2. In a large pot, add the rinsed rice and 3 cups of water. Place it on medium-high heat and bring to a boil. Once it starts boiling, reduce the heat to its lowest setting, cover, and let it simmer for approximately 35-40 minutes, or until the rice is tender and the water has been absorbed.

3. While the rice is cooking, if using fresh green beans, wash and chop them into small, bite-sized pieces. If using frozen, ensure they are thawed.

4. Using another skillet or pot, add the chopped green beans and a cup of water. Cook them over medium heat until they are tender. Drain the water once done.

5. Take the meat from the rotisserie chicken, ensuring all bones and skin are removed to make it safe for your dog. Shred or dice the chicken meat into bite-sized pieces.

6. Into the green beans, add the shredded chicken, diced mango, and shredded baby spinach. Stir well and cook on a medium heat just long enough for the spinach to wilt and the chicken to be warmed through, about 2-3 minutes.

7. By this time, your rice should be cooked. Fluff it with a fork and add it to the chicken and vegetable mixture, stirring well to combine all ingredients.

8. Let the medley cool to room temperature before serving to your pet. Store in the fridge in an airtight container for 2 - 3 days or in the freezer for 2 - 3 months.

Nutrition Information: Makes 12 portions (±1 cup each).

Calories: 219 kCal

Carbohydrate: 22.6g

Protein: 24.3g

Fat: 3.1g

BEEF AND APPLE CASSEROLE

Ingredients:

1½ cups (300 gms / 10.6 oz) brown rice, raw

1 Tbsp (15 ml / ½ fl oz) flaxseed oil

1 kg (4.4 lb.) lean ground beef

1 kg (2 lb.) carrots (grated)

1 kg (2 lb.) apple (grated)

2 cups (200 gms / 7 oz) cabbage (shredded)

Instructions

1. First, wash the brown rice under cold water using a fine-mesh sieve to remove excess starch. This helps prevent the rice from becoming too sticky.

2. In a large pot, combine the rinsed rice and 3 cups of water. Bring to a boil over medium-high heat. Once boiling, reduce heat to low, cover the pot, and let simmer for about 35-40 minutes, or until the rice is tender and water is absorbed.

3. In a separate large skillet, warm the flaxseed oil over medium heat. Add the ground beef, breaking it apart as it cooks. Cook until it's thoroughly browned and no longer pink.

4. Mix in the grated carrots and apples to the beef, stirring occasionally, and cook for another 5-7 minutes or until the carrots have softened slightly.

5. Introduce the shredded cabbage into the skillet, mixing well. Cook for an additional 5 minutes or until slightly softened.

6. After the rice is done, fluff it with a fork and incorporate it into the beef and vegetable mix. Stir until all ingredients are well combined.

7. Allow the mixture to cool to room temperature before serving to your dog. Store in the fridge in an airtight container for 2 - 3 days or in the freezer for 2 - 3 months.

Nutrition Information: Makes 14 portions (±1 cup each).

Calories: 261 kCal

Carbohydrate: 26.4g

Protein: 24.1g

Fat: 6.1g

CHICKEN WITH LENTILS

Ingredients

1 ½ cups (300 gms / 10.5 oz) orange split lentils

2 (120 gms / 4 oz) carrots (diced)

1 large (225 gms / ½ lb.) sweet potato (diced)

2 cups (160 gms / 5.6 oz) broccoli (chopped)

3 ½ cups (875 ml / 1.8 pints) water

900 gms (2 lb.) cooked chicken (shredded)

Instructions

1. Rinse the orange split lentils under cold water in a mesh strainer to remove any dirt or debris.

2. In a large pot or Dutch oven, combine the rinsed lentils, diced carrots, diced sweet potato, and chopped broccoli.

3. Pour in the 3 ½ cups of water to cover the ingredients.

4. Place the pot on medium-high heat and bring the mixture to a boil.

5. Once boiling, reduce the heat to low, cover the pot with a lid, and let it simmer for about 20-25 minutes or until the lentils and vegetables are tender.

6. While the lentils and vegetables are cooking, shred the cooked chicken into smaller, bite-sized pieces.

7. After the lentils and vegetables are tender, add the shredded cooked chicken to the pot. Stir to combine all the ingredients.

8. Continue to simmer the mixture on low heat for an additional 5-10 minutes to heat the chicken through.

9. Allow to cool before serving to your dog. Store in the fridge in an airtight container for 2 - 3 days or in the freezer for 2 - 3 months.

Nutrition Information: Makes 10 portions (±1 cup each).

Calories: 198 kCal

Carbohydrate: 13.5g

Protein: 29.8g

Fat: 3g

RABBIT AND CARROT STEW

Ingredients

1 Tbsp (15 ml/1 fl oz) flaxseed oil

1 (1.5 kg/3.3 lb.) rabbit

2 cups (1 liter/2 pints) water

1 cup (90 gms/3 oz) rolled oats, raw

2 (120 gms/4 oz) carrots (diced)

2 (160 gms/5.6 oz) apples (cored and diced)

⅓ cup (10 gms/0.4 oz) fresh parsley (chopped)

Instructions

1. Start by preparing the rabbit. Ensure it is cleaned and cut into suitable pieces for your dog's size. Remove all bones.

2. In a large pot or Dutch oven, heat the flaxseed oil over medium heat.

3. Add the rabbit pieces to the pot and sear them on all sides until they are lightly browned.

4. Pour in the 2 cups of water to cover the rabbit pieces.

5. Bring the mixture to a boil over high heat, then reduce the heat to low, cover the pot with a lid, and let it simmer for about 45-60 minutes or until the rabbit is fully cooked and tender.

6. While the rabbit is cooking, rinse the raw rolled oats under cold water to remove excess starch.

7. Once the rabbit is fully cooked, add the rinsed rolled oats, diced carrots, diced apples, and chopped fresh parsley to the pot. Stir to combine all the ingredients.

8. Continue to simmer the stew on low heat for an additional 15-20 minutes or until the oats are fully cooked and the carrots and apples are tender.

9. Store in the fridge in an airtight container for 2 - 3 days or in the freezer for 2 - 3 months.

Nutrition Information: Makes 18 portions (±1 cup each).

Calories: 214 kCal

Carbohydrate: 9.7g

Protein: 25.6g

Fat: 7.5g

TURKEY AND BROCCOLI BOWL

Ingredients

450 gms (1 lb.) turkey breast

4 cups (1 liter/2 pints) water

1½ cups (200 gms/7 oz) brown rice, raw

1 large (225 gms/½ lb.) sweet potato (diced)

1 teaspoon dried rosemary

2 (120 gms/4 oz) carrots (sliced)

450 gms (1 lb.) frozen broccoli florets

Instructions

1. Start by preparing the turkey breast. Ensure it is boneless and cut it into suitable pieces for your dog's size.

2. In a large pot or Dutch oven, combine the turkey pieces and 4 cups of water.

3. Place the pot on medium-high heat and bring the mixture to a boil.

4. Once boiling, reduce the heat to low, cover the pot with a lid, and let it simmer for about 15-20 minutes or until the turkey is fully cooked and tender. Remove the turkey from the pot and allow it to cool.

5. While the turkey is cooling, rinse the raw brown rice under cold water to remove excess starch.

6. In the same pot, add the rinsed brown rice, diced sweet potato, dried rosemary, and sliced carrots. Pour in enough water to cover the ingredients.

7. Bring the mixture to a boil over high heat, then reduce the heat to low, cover the pot, and let it simmer for about 20-25 minutes or until the rice and vegetables are tender.

8. While the rice and vegetables are cooking, shred the cooked turkey into smaller, bite-sized pieces.

9. Once the rice and vegetables are tender, add the frozen broccoli florets to the pot. Stir to combine all the ingredients.

10. Continue to simmer the mixture on low heat for an additional 5-10 minutes, or until the broccoli is heated through.

11. Allow to cool before serving to your dog. Store in the fridge in an airtight container for 2 - 3 days or in the freezer for 2 - 3 months.

Nutrition Information: Makes 8 portions (±1 cup each).

Calories: 237 kCal

Carbohydrate: 30.1g

Protein: 20.6g

Fat: 3.7g

CHICKEN AND CARROT STEW

Ingredients

1.4 kg (3 lb.) chicken thighs (skin and bones removed)

¼ cup (35 gms / 1.2 oz) chicken livers (diced)

2 (120 gms / 4 oz) carrots (sliced)

1 cup (175 gms / 6 oz) frozen corn

1 (180 gms / 6.3 oz) pear (cored, and chopped)

3 cups (750 ml / 1.6 pints) water

1 cup (160 gms / 5.6 oz) frozen green peas

⅓ cup fresh parsley (chopped)

Instructions

1. Start by preparing the turkey breast. Ensure it is boneless and cut it into suitable pieces for your dog's size.

2. In a large pot or Dutch oven, combine the turkey pieces and 4 cups of water.

3. Place the pot on medium-high heat and bring the mixture to a boil.

4. Once boiling, reduce the heat to low, cover the pot with a lid, and let it simmer for about 15-20 minutes or until the turkey is fully cooked and tender. Remove the turkey from the pot and allow it to cool.

5. While the turkey is cooling, rinse the raw brown rice under cold water to remove excess starch.

6. In the same pot, add the rinsed brown rice, diced sweet potato, dried rosemary, and sliced carrots. Pour in enough water to cover the ingredients.

7. Bring the mixture to a boil over high heat, then reduce the heat to low, cover the pot, and let it simmer for about 20-25 minutes or until the rice and vegetables are tender.

8. While the rice and vegetables are cooking, shred the cooked turkey into smaller, bite-sized pieces.

9. Once the rice and vegetables are tender, add the frozen broccoli florets to the pot. Stir to combine all the ingredients.

10. Continue to simmer the mixture on low heat for an additional 5-10 minutes, or until the broccoli is heated through.

11. Cool to room temperature before giving it to your dog. Store in the fridge in an airtight container for 2 - 3 days or in the freezer for 2 - 3 months.

Nutrition Information: Makes 6 portions (±1 cup each).

Calories: 231 kCal

Carbohydrate: 8.1g

Protein: 30.9g

Fat: 7.9g

CHICKEN WITH BLUEBERRIES

Ingredients

680 gms (1.5 lb.) chicken thighs (skin and bones removed)

4 cups (1 liter/2 pints) water

2 cups (400 gms/14 oz) Quinoa, raw

3 cups (480 gms/16.8 oz) frozen green peas

½ cup (90 gms/3.1 oz) yellow bell peppers (chopped)

1 cup (150 gms/5.2 oz) blueberries

Instructions

1. Start by removing the skin and bones from the chicken thighs. You can also use boneless, skinless chicken thighs if available.

2. In a large pot or Dutch oven, combine the boneless chicken thighs, diced chicken livers, sliced carrots, frozen corn, and chopped pear.

3. Pour in the 3 cups of water to cover the ingredients.

4. Place the pot on medium-high heat and bring the mixture to a boil.

5. Once boiling, reduce the heat to low, cover the pot with a lid, and let it simmer for about 20-25 minutes or until the chicken is fully cooked and tender.

6. While the chicken is simmering, rinse the frozen green peas under cold water to thaw them.

7. After the chicken is fully cooked, add the thawed green peas and chopped fresh parsley to the pot. Stir to combine all the ingredients.

8. Continue to simmer the stew on low heat for an additional 5-10 minutes to heat the peas and allow the flavors to meld.

9. Cool to room temperature before giving it to your dog. Store in the fridge in an airtight container for 2 - 3 days or in the freezer for 2 - 3 months.

Nutrition Information: Makes 12 portions (±1 cup each).

Calories: 250 kCal

Carbohydrate: 29.6g

Protein: 23.4g

Fat: 3.9g

PUP LOAF

Ingredients

450 gms (1 lb.) ground chicken
2 eggs (lightly beaten)
1 cup (135 gms / 4.5 oz) rolled oats, raw
1 apple (80 gms / 28 0z) (peeled, cored, and grated)
1 cup (110 gms / 3.9 oz) carrot (grated)
½ cup (80 gms / 2.8 oz) cottage cheese

Variations:

Replace the ground chicken with any of the following:

- 450 gms (1 lb.) ground beef, lean
- 450 gms (1 lb.) ground turkey
- 450 gms (1 lb.) fish such as salmon (raw and finely chopped)
- Replace ⅓ of the meat (150g/5.3oz) with 150 gms (5.3 oz) of beef liver, chicken liver, or beef heart.

Replace the rolled oats with any of the following:

- 350 gms (12.3 oz) sweet potato (cooked and mashed)
- 250 gms (8.8 oz) potato (cooked and mashed)
- 1 ½ cups (300 gms / 10.6 oz) rice (cooked)

Replace the apple with any of the following:

- 1 (170 gms / 6 oz) pear (peeled, cored, and grated)
- 1 (120 gms / 4.2 oz) banana (peeled and mashed)
- ½ cup (60 gms / 2.1 oz) berries of your choice (cleaned and mashed)

Replace the carrot with any of the following vegetables:

- 175 gms (6.2 oz) broccoli (washed and grated)
- 100 gms (3.5 oz) cabbage (finely shredded)
- 160 gms (5.6 oz) spinach (finely shredded)

- 200 gms (7 oz) butternut squash(cooked and mashed)
- 130 gms (4.6 oz) beets (cooked and grated)

Instructions

1. Preheat your oven to 180°C (350°F) and grease a loaf pan suitable for the size of your pup loaf.

2. In a large mixing bowl, combine the ground chicken, lightly beaten eggs, and raw rolled oats. Mix them together until well combined.

3. Peel, core, and grate the apple. Grate the carrots as well.

4. Add the grated apple, grated carrots, and cottage cheese to the chicken mixture. Mix everything thoroughly to ensure an even distribution of ingredients.

5. Transfer the mixture into the greased loaf pan, pressing it down to ensure it fills the pan evenly.

6. Place the loaf pan in the preheated oven and bake for approximately 45-60 minutes, or until the pup loaf is fully cooked and has a golden brown top.

7. Remove the pup loaf from the oven and allow it to cool in the pan for a few minutes.

8. Once cooled slightly, carefully remove the pup loaf from the pan and let it cool completely on a wire rack.

9. Once completely cool, slice the pup loaf into portions appropriate for your dog's size.

10. Store sliced pup loaf in the fridge in an airtight container for 2 - 3 days or in the freezer for 2 - 3 months. When freezing, separate the slices with parchment paper.

Nutrition Information for Original Recipe: Makes 8 thick slices.

Calories: 213 kCal

Carbohydrate: 16.3g

Protein: 21.4g

Fat: 6.6g

CHAPTER 12
MAINS WITH SEAFOOD

Treat your furry best friend to a seafood dinner. Not only do these seafood recipes taste great, but they are a source of essential nutrients, such as omega-3 fatty acids, to keep your dog's coat soft and shiny, their eyes bright, and their brain sharp.

Choose between salmon, tuna, cod, white fish, sardines, shrimp, and crab combined with healthy grains and dog-friendly fruits and vegetables to create delectable doggie dishes.

Recipe notes:

1. Fish bones can be dangerous for both people and dogs. Ensure that all the bones are removed from the fish before adding them to your recipes.

2. Fish bones such as those in canned sardines are soft are usually safe for dogs to consume. However, it is suggested that you err on the side of caution and avoid all fish bones in your homemade dog food.

3. Ensure to regularly check with your dog's veterinarian when transitioning them onto a homemade dog food diet. Since many human foods are toxic to dogs, it's not always possible to meet their nutrient requirements from food alone. Ask your vet to recommend a nutrition supplement if your dog is showing signs of poor nutrition.

4. The nutritional value for each recipe is an estimate based on the recipe analysis (Recipe Calorie and Nutrition Calculator, n.d.). The exact values depend on the size of the portions, and, in some cases, the brand of ingredients used.

SALMON AND POTATO HASH

Ingredients

1 (60 gms / 2 oz) carrot (grated)

1 cup (100gms / 3.5 oz) cabbage (shredded)

225 gms (8oz) salmon, raw (chopped)*

2 eggs (lightly beaten)

2 (310 gms / 11 oz) potatoes (peeled, cubed, and boiled)

½ cup (100 gms / 3.5 oz) butternut squash (peeled, cubed, and boiled)

*(Canned salmon can be used instead)

Instructions

1. Start by preparing the ingredients. Grate the carrot, shred the cabbage, chop the raw salmon (or open and drain canned salmon if using), peel, cube, and boil the potatoes and butternut squash until they are soft. Drain and let them cool.

2. In a large mixing bowl, lightly beat the eggs.

3. Add the grated carrot, shredded cabbage, chopped salmon (or canned salmon), and the cooked and cooled potatoes and butternut squash to the beaten eggs.

4. Mix all the ingredients together until well combined.

5. Heat a non-stick skillet or frying pan over medium heat and lightly grease it with a small amount of cooking oil.

6. Scoop portions of the salmon and potato mixture into the skillet, forming small patties or hash browns with your hands.

7. Cook the patties for about 3-4 minutes on each side, or until they are cooked through and have a nice golden brown color.

8. Remove the patties from the skillet and let them cool for a few minutes before serving them to your dog. Store in the fridge in an airtight container for 2 - 3 days or in the freezer for 2 - 3 months.

Nutrition Information: Makes 8 portions (±1 cup each).

Calories: 178 kCal

Carbohydrate: 16.7g

Protein: 15.7g

Fat: 5.8g

WHITEFISH AND QUINOA DELIGHT

Ingredients

2.7 kg (6 lb.) white fish fillets

2 cups (400 gms / 14 oz) quinoa, raw

3 medium (600 gms / 21 oz) zucchini (washed and grated)

1 cup (150 gms / 5.3 oz) frozen green beans

4 medium (240 gms / 8 oz) carrots (grated)

2 cups (500 gms / 17.6 oz) pumpkin (cubed and boiled)

Instructions

1. Begin by preparing the ingredients. Wash and grate the zucchini, grate the carrots, and cube the pumpkin. Set these aside.

2. Rinse the quinoa under cold water to remove excess starch.

3. In a large pot, bring 4 cups of water to a boil. Add the rinsed quinoa to the boiling water.

4. Reduce the heat to low, cover the pot, and let the quinoa simmer for about 15-20 minutes, or until it's cooked and the water is absorbed. Remove from heat and let it cool.

5. While the quinoa is cooking, prepare the whitefish fillets. You can either bake, steam, or poach them until they are fully cooked. Once cooked, let the fish cool and then flake it into small pieces.

6. In a large mixing bowl, combine the cooked quinoa, grated zucchini, grated carrots, and flaked whitefish. Mix these ingredients together.

7. Add the frozen green beans and the cubed and boiled pumpkin to the mixture. Stir until everything is well combined.

8. Allow to cool before serving to your dog. Store in the fridge in an airtight container for 2 - 3 days or in the freezer for 2 - 3 months.

Nutrition Information: Makes 20 portions (±1 cup each).

Calories: 200kCal

Carbohydrate: 17.6g

Protein: 27.1g

Fat: 2.6g

SARDINE AND CARROT STIR-FRY

Ingredients

1 (60 gms/2 oz) carrot (grated)

1 cup (100 gms/3.5 oz) cabbage (shredded)

½ cup (80 gms/2.8 oz) frozen green peas

1 cup (30 gms/1.1 oz) baby spinach (shredded)

1 can (105 gms/3.75 oz) sardines in water (drained and bones removed)

1 cup (200 gms/7 oz) brown rice (cooked)

Instructions

1. Start by preparing the ingredients. Grate the carrot, shred the cabbage, and shred the baby spinach. Set these aside.

2. In a medium-sized pot, cook the brown rice according to the package instructions. Once cooked, let it cool.

3. Drain the sardines in water and remove any bones. Flake the sardines into small pieces.

4. In a large non-stick skillet or wok, heat a small amount of water or low-sodium broth over medium heat.

5. Add the grated carrot, shredded cabbage, frozen green peas, and shredded baby spinach to the skillet. Stir-fry these vegetables for about 3-4 minutes, or until they begin to soften.

6. Add the flaked sardines to the skillet and continue stir-frying for another 2-3 minutes or until everything is heated through.

7. Add the cooked brown rice to the skillet and mix it with the vegetables and sardines. Stir-fry for an additional 2-3 minutes to ensure everything is well combined.

8. Allow to cool before serving to your dog. Store in the fridge in an airtight container for 2 - 3 days or in the freezer for 2 - 3 months.

Nutrition Information: Makes 2 meals.

Calories: 273 kCal

Carbohydrate: 34.1g

Protein: 18.5g

Fat: 7g*

*Note the high fat content. Include this recipe in your dog's meal plan as a special treat. It should not be a regular meal.

COD AND SPINACH MEDLEY

Ingredients

2 eggs

½ cup (100 gms / 3.5 oz) brown rice, raw

900 gms (2 lb.) cod fillets

3 medium (600 gmd / 21 oz) zucchini (washed and diced)

1 stalk of celery

1 cup (175 gms / 5.8 oz) frozen corn

1 cup (30 gms / 1.1 oz) baby spinach (chopped)

Instructions

1. Begin by preparing the ingredients. Dice the zucchini, chop the baby spinach, and dice the celery. Set these aside.

2. In a medium-sized pot, bring 1 cup of water to a boil. Add the brown rice to the boiling water.

3. Reduce the heat to low, cover the pot, and let the rice simmer for about 15-20 minutes, or until it's cooked and the water is absorbed. Remove from heat and let it cool.

4. While the rice is cooking, prepare the cod. You can either bake, steam, or poach it until it's fully cooked. Once cooked, let the cod cool and then break it into small pieces.

5. In a large mixing bowl, beat the eggs.

6. Add the diced zucchini, chopped baby spinach, diced celery, frozen corn, and the cooked and cooled cod to the beaten eggs. Mix these ingredients together.

7. Add the cooked brown rice to the mixture and stir until everything is well combined.

8. Allow to cool before serving to your dog. Store in the fridge in an airtight container for 2 - 3 days or in the freezer for 2 - 3 months.

Nutrition Information: Makes 10 portions (±1 cup each).

Calories: 167 kCal

Carbohydrate: 12.8g

Protein: 23.7g

Fat: 2.2g

SHRIMP AND PEA PILAF

Ingredients

1 cup (200 gms / 7 oz) brown rice, raw

½ (125 gms / 4.4 oz) fennel bulb (diced)

450 gms (1 lb.) shrimp (ground in a food processor)

1 can (340 gms / 12 oz) tuna, canned in water

1 cup (160 gms / 5.6 oz) frozen green peas

½ cup (125 ml / 4.2 fl oz) plain low-fat yogurt

Instructions

1. Begin by preparing the ingredients. Dice the fennel bulb and set it aside.

2. In a medium-sized pot, bring 2 cups of water to a boil. Add the brown rice to the boiling water.

3. Reduce the heat to low, cover the pot, and let the rice simmer for about 40-45 minutes, or until it's cooked and the water is absorbed. Remove from heat and let it cool.

4. While the rice is cooking, prepare the shrimp. Ground the shrimp in a food processor until it reaches a finely minced consistency.

5. In a large mixing bowl, combine the ground shrimp, diced fennel, canned tuna (with water drained), frozen green peas, and plain low-fat yogurt. Mix these ingredients together.

6. Once the cooked brown rice has cooled, add it to the mixture and stir until everything is well combined.

7. Allow to cool before serving to your dog. Store in the fridge in an airtight container for 2 - 3 days or in the freezer for 2 - 3 months.

Nutrition Information: Makes 10 portions (±1 cup each).

Calories: 215 kCal

Carbohydrate: 20g

Protein: 22.5g

Fat: 4.3g

TUNA AND SWEET POTATO MASH

Ingredients

2 large (500 gms/1 lb.) sweet potato (diced)

2 (160 gms/5.6 oz) apples (cored and diced)

225 gms (8oz) fresh tuna

225 gms (8oz) white fish

450 gms (1 lb.) frozen broccoli florets

Instructions

1. Begin by preparing the ingredients. Dice the sweet potatoes and apples, and set them aside.

2. In a large pot, bring 4 cups of water to a boil. Add the diced sweet potatoes and apples to the boiling water.

3. Reduce the heat to a simmer and let the sweet potatoes and apples cook for about 15-20 minutes, or until they are tender and can be easily pierced with a fork. Drain any excess water and let them cool.

4. While the sweet potatoes and apples are cooking, prepare the fresh tuna and white fish. You can either bake, steam, or poach them until they are fully cooked. Once cooked, let them cool.

5. Once the cooked sweet potatoes, apples, tuna, and white fish have cooled, place them in a food processor or blender.

6. Blend the ingredients until you have a smooth mash consistency. You may need to add a small amount of water to achieve the desired texture.

7. In a separate pot, steam the frozen broccoli florets until they are tender and bright green.

8. Mix the steamed broccoli into the tuna and sweet potato mash..

9. Allow to cool before serving to your dog. Store in the fridge in an airtight container for 2 - 3 days or in the freezer for 2 - 3 months.

Nutrition Information: Makes 12 portions (±1 cup each).

Calories: 231 kCal

Carbohydrate: 30.4g

Protein: 20.4g

Fat: 3.9g

TROUT AND GREEN BEAN BOWL

Ingredients

450 gms (1 lb.) trout (bones removed)

450 gms (1 lb.) frozen green beans

450 gms (1 lb.) potato (cleaned and diced)

1 cup (30 gms / 1.1 oz) baby spinach (shredded)

Instructions

1. Begin by preparing the ingredients. Clean and dice the potato, and set it aside.

2. In a large pot, bring 4 cups of water to a boil. Add the diced potatoes to the boiling water.

3. Reduce the heat to a simmer and let the potatoes cook for about 10-15 minutes, or until they are tender and can be easily pierced with a fork. Drain any excess water and let them cool.

4. While the potatoes are cooking, prepare the trout. Ensure that all bones are removed, and the fish is ready for your dog to eat.

5. Steam or boil the frozen green beans until they are tender. Drain any excess water and let them cool.

6. Once the cooked potatoes, green beans, and trout have cooled, place them in a mixing bowl.

7. Mix these ingredients together thoroughly.

8. Add the shredded baby spinach to the bowl and mix it into the mixture.

9. Allow to cool before serving to your dog. Store in the fridge in an airtight container for 2 - 3 days or in the freezer for 2 - 3 months.

Nutrition Information: Makes 6 portions (±1 cup each).

Calories: 225 kCal

Carbohydrate: 18.6g

Protein: 23g

Fat: 6.5g

SARDINE AND ZUCCHINI DELIGHT

Ingredients

¼ cup (50 gms / 1.8 oz) rice, raw

1 can (105 gms / 3.75 oz) sardines in water (drained and bones removed)

1 medium (60 gms / 2 oz) carrot (diced)

1 medium (200 gms / 7 oz) zucchini (washed and diced)

Instructions

1. Start by preparing the rice. In a small saucepan, add ½ cup of water and bring it to a boil. Add the raw rice to the boiling water.

2. Reduce the heat to a simmer, cover the saucepan, and let the rice cook for about 15-20 minutes, or until it is tender and the water is absorbed. Once cooked, remove it from heat and let it cool.

3. While the rice is cooking, open the can of sardines packed in water and drain any excess liquid. Be sure to remove any bones.

4. Dice the carrot and zucchini into small pieces.

5. Once the rice, sardines, carrot, and zucchini have cooled, place them in a mixing bowl.

6. Mix these ingredients together thoroughly.

7. Allow to cool before serving to your dog. Store in the fridge in an airtight container for 2 - 3 days or in the freezer for 2 - 3 months.

Nutrition Information: Makes 2 meals.

Calories: 229 kCal

Carbohydrate: 26.3g

Protein: 16.2g

Fat: 6.4g

HALIBUT AND BROCCOLI STIR-FRY

Ingredients

1 cup (200 gms / 7 oz) pearl barley, raw

3 eggs

900 gms (2 lb.) halibut fillets (bones removed)

3 cups (525 gms / 18.5 oz) broccoli (cut into florets)

Instructions:

1. Start by preparing the pearl barley. In a medium saucepan, add 2 cups of water and bring it to a boil. Add the raw pearl barley to the boiling water.

2. Reduce the heat to a simmer, cover the saucepan, and let the barley cook for about 30-40 minutes, or until it is tender and the water is absorbed. Once cooked, remove it from heat and let it cool.

3. While the barley is cooking, crack the eggs into a bowl and lightly beat them.

4. Cut the halibut fillets into small, bite-sized pieces, ensuring that all bones are removed.

5. In a large skillet or wok, heat a small amount of oil over medium-high heat.

6. Add the halibut pieces to the skillet and stir-fry them for about 3-5 minutes, or until they are cooked through and lightly browned. Remove them from the skillet and set them aside to cool.

7. In the same skillet, add the broccoli florets and stir-fry them for about 5-7 minutes, or until they are tender and slightly crispy. You can add a splash of water to help steam the broccoli if needed.

8. Once the barley, halibut, and broccoli have cooled, place them in a mixing bowl.

9. Pour the beaten eggs over the mixture and gently toss everything together..

10. Allow to cool before serving to your dog. Store in the fridge in an airtight container for 2 - 3 days, or in the freezer for 2 - 3 months.

Nutrition Information: Makes 8 portions (±1 cup each).

Calories: 195 kCal

Carbohydrate: 16g

Protein: 24.6g

Fat: 3.2g

CRAB AND SWEET CORN MEDLEY

Ingredients

1.4 kg (3 lb.) potatoes (washed and diced)

8 ears fresh corn (cooked and corn kernels removed)

or 6 cups (1 kg/2.2 lb.) of frozen corn

1.4 kg (3 lb.) ground shrimp meat

Instructions

1. Start by preparing the potatoes. Wash and dice them into small, bite-sized pieces.

2. If using fresh corn, cook the corn ears until they are tender. Once cooked, remove the corn kernels from the cobs. If using frozen corn, thaw it.

3. In a large skillet or pot, add a small amount of water and bring it to a simmer.

4. Add the diced potatoes to the simmering water and cook them for about 15-20 minutes, or until they are soft and easily pierced with a fork. Drain the potatoes and let them cool.

5. In a separate large mixing bowl, combine the ground shrimp meat and corn kernels.

6. Add the cooked and cooled diced potatoes to the shrimp and corn mixture.

7. Gently toss all the ingredients together to create a medley.

8. Allow to cool before serving to your dog. Store in the fridge in an airtight container for 2 - 3 days or in the freezer for 2 - 3 months.

Nutrition Information: Makes 12 portions (±1 cup each).

Calories: 230 kCal

Carbohydrate: 22.5g

Protein: 29g

Fat: 2.3g

SHRIMP AND SPINACH RICE

Ingredients

1 cup (200g/70oz) Brown rice, raw

1 Tbsp (15 ml/0.5 fl oz) flaxseed oil

450 gms (1 lb.) ground shrimp meat

2 cups (60 gms/2.2 oz) baby spinach (chopped)

2 medium (120 gms/4 oz) carrots (Grated)

½ tsp (2.5 ml/0.1 fl oz) ground turmeric

1 egg (lightly beaten)

Instructions

1. Start by cooking the brown rice. In a saucepan, combine the raw brown rice with the appropriate amount of water according to package instructions. Cook the rice until it's tender and all the water is absorbed. Let it cool completely.

2. While the rice is cooking, you can prepare the other ingredients. Grate the carrots and chop the baby spinach.

3. In a large skillet or pan, heat the flaxseed oil over medium heat.

4. Add the ground shrimp meat to the skillet and cook it until it's thoroughly cooked and no longer pink, breaking it into smaller pieces as it cooks.

5. Stir in the grated carrots and chopped baby spinach. Cook for an additional 5-7 minutes until the vegetables are tender.

6. Add the cooked brown rice to the skillet with the shrimp and vegetables.

7. Sprinkle the ground turmeric over the mixture and stir it in. Turmeric is a healthy spice for dogs and can add flavor and potential health benefits.

8. Push the rice and shrimp mixture to one side of the skillet, creating an empty space on the other side.

9. Pour the lightly beaten egg into the empty space and scramble it until it's fully cooked.

10. Mix the scrambled egg into the rice and shrimp mixture, ensuring it's evenly distributed.

11. Allow to cool before serving to your dog. Store in the fridge in an airtight container for 2 - 3 days, or in the freezer for 2 - 3 months.

Nutrition Information: Makes 6 portions (±1 cup each).

Calories: 253 kCal   Carbohydrate: 28.9g

Protein: 21g   Fat: 5.3g

HADDOCK AND CARROT CASSEROLE

Ingredients

4 cups (1 liter/2.1 pints) water

3 medium (180 gms/6 oz) carrots (sliced)

3 (330 gms/12 oz) parsnips (grated)

1 (900 gms/2 lb.) small cabbage (chopped)

300 gms (10.6 oz)) green beans

2 kg (2.2 lb.) frozen haddock fillets

2 cups (160 gms/5.6 oz) rolled oats

Instructions

1. Preheat your oven to 180°C (350°F).

2. Start by boiling the carrots, parsnips, cabbage, and green beans in the 4 cups of water until they are tender. This usually takes about 15-20 minutes. Drain the vegetables and let them cool.

3. While the vegetables are cooling, thaw the frozen haddock if it's not already thawed. You can do this by placing it in the refrigerator for a few hours or using the defrost function on your microwave.

4. Once the vegetables have cooled, combine them with the rolled oats in a large mixing bowl. The oats will help bind the casserole together.

5. Flake the haddock into small pieces and add it to the mixing bowl with the vegetables and oats. Mix everything together thoroughly.

6. Transfer the mixture into a greased casserole dish, spreading it out evenly.

7. Place the casserole dish in the preheated oven and bake for about 30-35 minutes or until the top is golden brown and the casserole is heated through.

8. Allow to cool before serving to your dog. Store in the fridge in an airtight container for 2 - 3 days or in the freezer for 2 - 3 months.

Nutrition Information: Makes 12 portions (±1 cup each).

Calories: 189 kCal

Carbohydrate: 25.9g

Protein: 18.8g

Fat: 2g

TUNA WITH NOODLES

Ingredients

450 gms (1 lb.) egg noodles

175 gms (6.2 oz) frozen broccoli florets

170 gms (6 oz) tuna (canned in water)

¼ cup (80 ml/2.7 fl oz) low-fat cottage cheese

¼ cup (30 gms/1 oz) reduced-fat cheddar cheese (grated)

Instructions

1. Start by cooking the egg noodles according to the package instructions. Drain and set aside.

2. Steam or boil the frozen broccoli florets until they are tender. Drain and set aside.

3. In a large mixing bowl, combine the cooked egg noodles, steamed broccoli, canned tuna (drained), low-fat cottage cheese, and reduced-fat cheddar cheese.

4. Mix all the ingredients together thoroughly, ensuring that the cheese is evenly distributed.

5. Allow to cool before serving to your dog. Store in the fridge in an airtight container for 2 - 3 days, or in the freezer for 2 - 3 months.

Nutrition Information: Makes 4 portions (±1 cup each).

Calories: 279 kCal

Carbohydrate: 32.1g

Protein: 22.1g

Fat: 6.8g

FISH PUP LOAF

Ingredients

350 gms (12.3 oz) sweet potato (cooked and mashed)

2 cans (500 gms/1.1 lb.) salmon in water

1 cup (80 gms/2.8 oz) oat flour (make your own by placing 1 cup of rolled oats in a blender)

1 egg (lightly beaten)

1 medium (60 gms/2 oz) carrot (grated)

1 stalk of celery (finely chopped)

½ tsp parsley (finely chopped)

1 Tbsp (15 ml/0.5 fl oz) plain low-fat yogurt

Variations:

Replace the canned salmon with any of the following:

- 500 gms (1.1 lb.) tuna (canned in water)
- 500 gms (1.1 lb.) fresh Salmon (finely chopped)
- 500 gms (1.1 lb.) fresh tuna (finely chopped)
- 500 gms (1.1 lb.) white fish (finely chopped)
- 500 gms (1.1 lb.) sardines (canned in water)
- 500 gms (1.1 lb.) shrimp (ground)

Replace the sweet potato with any of the following:

- 250g (8.8oz) Potato (cooked and mashed)
- 1 ½ cups (300g/10.6oz) Rice (cooked)
- 1 ½ cups (300g/10.6oz) Quinoa (cooked)

Replace the carrot with any of the following vegetables:

- 175 gms (6.2 oz) broccoli (washed and grated)
- 100 gms (3.5 oz) cabbage (finely shredded)
- 160 gms (5.6 oz) spinach (finely shredded)

- 200 gms (7 oz) butternut squash (cooked and mashed)
- 130 gms (4.6 oz) Beets (cooked and grated)

Instructions

1. Preheat your oven to 180°C (350°F) and grease a loaf pan with a bit of oil or cooking spray.

2. In a large mixing bowl, combine the cooked and mashed sweet potato, canned salmon (including the liquid), oat flour (made by blending rolled oats), and the lightly beaten egg. Mix these ingredients thoroughly until well combined.

3. Add the grated carrot, finely chopped celery, and finely chopped parsley to the mixture. Stir to evenly distribute these ingredients throughout the mixture.

4. Transfer the prepared mixture into the greased loaf pan, spreading it out evenly.

5. Bake in the preheated oven for about 30-35 minutes, or until the loaf is set and the top is golden brown.

6. Remove the loaf from the oven and allow it to cool completely in the pan.

7. Once cooled, you can cut the pup loaf into slices or cubes, depending on your dog's size and preferences.

8. For an extra treat, you can spread a thin layer of plain low-fat yogurt on top of the slices before serving.

9. Store sliced fish pup loaf in the fridge in an airtight container for 2 - 3 days or in the freezer for 2 - 3 months. When freezing, separate the slices with parchment paper.

Nutrition Information for Original Recipe: Makes 6 thick slices.

Calories: 230 kCal

Carbohydrate: 22.4g

Protein: 20.3g

Fat: 6.9g

CHAPTER 13
VEGETARIAN/VEGAN MAINS

While most dogs prefer meaty dishes, many thrive on well balanced vegan meals. Just like humans, including meat-free dishes in your dog's meal plan offers health benefits due to the lower fat and higher fiber content.

It is crucial to remember that most plant-based protein foods are incomplete. In other words, they don't provide all the essential amino acids, and a variety of legumes, grains, and vegetables must be served to ensure your pet's protein requirements are being met.

Recipe notes:

1. Beans and chickpeas must be soaked overnight before being cooked. All of the recipes in this chapter refer to cooked portions.

2. A canine vegan diet requires careful planning to ensure their nutritional needs are met. Protein and fat may be lacking in their diet. Talk to your vet about recommendations for a nutrition supplement if your dog is showing signs of poor nutrition.

3. The nutritional value for each recipe is an estimate based on the recipe analysis (Recipe Calorie and Nutrition Calculator, n.d.). The exact values depend on the size of the portions, and, in some cases, the brand of ingredients used.

TOFU WITH BLACK-EYED PEAS AND RICE

Ingredients

1 cup (195 gms/6.9 oz) cooked brown rice

1 cup (250 gms/8.8 oz) firm tofu, drained and cubed

1 cup (170 gms/6 oz) cooked black-eyed peas

1 small (about 60 gms/2.1 oz) carrot, finely chopped

1/2 cup (approximately 72 gms/2.5 oz) peas (fresh or frozen) 1 tablespoon (15 ml/0.5 oz) olive oil or flaxseed oil

1/4 teaspoon ground seaweed (optional, for minerals)

Instructions

1. If using dried black-eyed peas, soak them overnight. Drain, rinse and then cook until they're soft. If using canned, ensure they're free of salt and other additives, and rinse them thoroughly.

2. Cook the brown rice as per the package instructions or use pre-cooked brown rice.

3. Add the cubed tofu and sauté until they turn a light golden color, turning occasionally to ensure even cooking.

4. When the rice is cooked, drain off any excess water and return the pot to the stove.

5. Stir in the black-eyed peas, tofu, ground seaweed, carrots and flaxseed oil. Continue cooking for another 5 – 7 minutes until the black-eyed peas are heated and the carrots are soft but not mushy.

6. Allow to cool before serving to your dog. Store in the fridge in an airtight container for 2 - 3 days, or in the freezer for 2 - 3 months.

Nutrition Information: Makes 8 portions (±1 cup each).

Calories: 200 kCal

Carbohydrate: 38.3g

Protein: 9.4g

Fat: 3.9g

PUMPKIN AND BROWN RICE BOWL

Ingredients:

½ cup (100 gms/3.5 oz) white rice, raw

½ cup (100 gms/3.5 oz) split orange lentils

1 cup (125 gms/4.4 oz) pumpkin (cubed)

¼ cup (80 ml/2.7 fl oz) low-fat cottage cheese

Instructions

1. Boil the rice, lentils, and pumpkin in a large pot over medium heat until they are cooked.

2. Drain off any excess water and stir in the cottage cheese.

3. Allow to cool before serving to your dog. Store in the fridge in an airtight container for 2 - 3 days, or in the freezer for 2 - 3 months.

Nutrition Information: Makes 4 portions (±1 cup each).

Calories: 212 kCal

Carbohydrate: 38.2g

Protein: 11.9g

Fat: 1g

BEAN AND CARROT CASSEROLE

Ingredients

2 Tbsp (30 ml / 1 oz) Canola oil

½ (125 gms / 4.4 oz) fennel bulb (diced)

1 stalk of celery

⅔ cup (130 gms / 4.6 oz) brown rice, raw

3 cups (750 ml / 1.6 pints) water

1 large (250 gms / 8.8 oz)) sweet potato (diced)

4 medium (240 gms / 8 oz) carrots (sliced)

425 gms (15 oz) black beans (soaked and cooked)

Instructions

1. In a large ovenproof casserole dish, heat the canola oil over medium heat.

2. Add the diced fennel bulb and sliced celery to the casserole dish. Sauté for a few minutes until they begin to soften.

3. Stir in the raw brown rice and cook for an additional 2-3 minutes, allowing the rice to become lightly toasted.

4. Pour in the water and bring the mixture to a boil. Reduce the heat to low, cover the dish, and simmer for about 30 minutes or until the rice is partially cooked.

5. While the rice is cooking, preheat your oven to 180°C (350°F).

6. After the rice has partially cooked, add the diced sweet potato, sliced carrots, and cooked black beans to the casserole dish. Stir well to combine all the ingredients.

7. Cover the casserole dish and transfer it to the preheated oven.

8. Bake for about 30-40 minutes or until the vegetables are tender, and the rice is fully cooked. Check the casserole periodically and add a bit more water if needed to prevent it from drying out.

9. Once done, remove the casserole from the oven and let it cool before serving. Store in the fridge in an airtight container for 2 - 3 days,or in the freezer for 2 - 3 months.

Nutrition Information: Makes portions (±1 cup each).

Calories: 254 kCal

Carbohydrate: 44.9g

Protein: 11g

Fat: 3.9g

CHICKPEA CAULIFLOWER BOWL WITH GREEN BEANS

Ingredients

2 Tbsp (30 ml / 1 oz) Canola oil

3 cups (255 gms / 9 oz) cauliflower (chopped)

1 cup (160 gms / 5.6 oz) frozen green beans

1 cup can (425 gms / 15 oz) chickpeas (drained and rinsed)

½ (125 ml / 4.2 fl oz) plain low-fat yogurt

Instructions

1. Heat the canola oil in a large skillet or pan over medium heat.

2. Add the chopped cauliflower to the pan and sauté for about 5-7 minutes, or until it starts to turn golden brown and becomes tender.

3. Stir in the frozen green beans and continue cooking for an additional 3-5 minutes, or until they are heated through and tender.

4. Add the drained and rinsed chickpeas to the skillet. Cook for an additional 2-3 minutes, stirring occasionally, until the chickpeas are heated.

5. Remove the skillet from heat and let the mixture cool slightly.

6. Once the mixture has cooled, stir in the plain low-fat yogurt until everything is well coated and combined. Store in the fridge in an airtight container for 2 - 3 days or in the freezer for 2 - 3 months.

Nutrition Information: Makes 4 portions (±1 cup each).

Calories: 250 kCal

Protein: 12.2g

Carbohydrate: 36.5g

Fat: 7g

BANANA AND QUINOA CONCOCTION

Ingredients

1 large (250 gms/8.8 oz)) sweet potato (diced)
¾ cup (125 gms/5.3 oz) quinoa, raw
1⅓ cups (330 gms/11.2 fl oz) water
1 cup (175 gms/6.2 oz) frozen broccoli florets
1 can (425 gms/15 oz) chickpeas (drained and rinsed)
1 (120 gms/4.2oz) Banana sliced

Instructions

1. Preheat the oven to 200°C (400°F).

2. Poke holes in the sweet potato with a fork, place it on a baking tray and bake it until tender, about 45 minutes to an hour.

3. In the meantime, cook the quinoa. Place the quinoa and water in a pot, bring to the boil over medium heat and simmer for 20 minutes, or until all the water has been absorbed.

4. Add the broccoli and chickpeas to the quinoa 5 minutes before the end of the cooking time to heat through.

5. Cut the cooked sweet potato into cubes and slice the banana. Add them to the quinoa mixture and stir to combine.

6. Allow to cool before serving to your dog. Store in the fridge in an airtight container for 2 - 3 days or in the freezer for 2 - 3 months.

Nutrition Information: Makes 6 portions (±1 cup each).

Calories: 241 kCal

Carbohydrate: 43g

Protein: 11.1g

Fat: 3.5g

POTATO AND LENTIL STEW

Ingredients

2 Tbsp (30 ml / 1 oz) Canola oil

3 medium (180 gms / 6oz) carrots (sliced)

250 gms (8.8 oz) potato (cubed)

4 cups (1 liter / 2.1 pints) vegetable stock (refer to recipe for Mixed Vegetable Stock in Chapter 10)

1¼ cups (250 gms / 8.8 oz) green lentils, raw

½ teaspoon dried oregano

1 Tbsp fresh parsley (chopped)

Instructions

1. In a large pot or Dutch oven, heat the canola oil over medium heat.

2. Add the sliced carrots and cook for about 3-5 minutes, or until they begin to soften.

3. Stir in the cubed potatoes and continue to cook for another 2-3 minutes.

4. Pour in the vegetable stock, ensuring that the carrots and potatoes are fully covered. If needed, you can adjust the amount of stock accordingly.

5. Add the green lentils and dried oregano to the pot.

6. Stir the mixture well, bring it to a boil, and then reduce the heat to low. Cover the pot and simmer for about 30-40 minutes, or until the lentils are tender and the stew has thickened. You may need to adjust the cooking time and add more stock if necessary.

7. Once the stew is ready, remove it from heat and stir in the fresh parsley.

8. Allow to cool before serving to your dog. Store in the fridge in an airtight container for 2 - 3 days or in the freezer for 2 - 3 months.

Nutrition Information: Makes 6 portions (±1 cup each).

Calories: 233 kCal

Carbohydrate: 35.3g

Protein: 11.8g

Fat: 5.2g

CHAPTER 14
SPECIAL DIET OPTIONS

As humans, we know that what we eat affects our health, and sometimes, our health issues determine what is best for us to eat. The same is true for dogs. Not only do they have unique dietary needs based on their size, breed, and age, but, if they suffer from chronic health conditions, such as digestive issues and diabetes, you may need to adapt their diet to meet their nutritional requirements.

Poor health is not the only thing to consider when considering special diet options for your four-legged friend. Their activity level, food allergies, and their weight must also be taken into account when planning their meals.

Veterinarian-formulated kibble is available in a wide range of products tailored to meet the needs of some of the most common health conditions that affect dogs. You can buy breed-specific, health condition-specific, weight loss, and allergy formulations to ensure your pet gets everything they need from their diet.

As unique as each formulation is, the food may not be ideal for your dog. Fortunately, homemade dog food can be fine-tuned to meet your dog's specific requirements. You can easily adapt the calorie, protein, fat, and carbohydrate content, and use a variety of dog-friendly fruits and vegetables to increase the vitamin and mineral content. Vitamin, mineral, and essential fatty acid supplements can also be added to your lovingly prepared doggie meals to ensure they are eating a diet that meets their unique needs.

This chapter briefly covers the special dietary options for specific health requirements, activity levels, digestive issues, food allergies, and weight management.

Diets Customized to Address Specific Health Requirements

There are several health conditions in dogs that require special dietary management. Some of the common health conditions that benefit from customized dietary management include:

Pancreatitis: A high dietary fat content can cause pancreatitis in dogs (Cridge et al., 2022). Therefore, dogs with pancreatitis should be fed a low-fat diet to reduce inflammation and minimize the risk of flare-ups.

Diabetes: It is critical to control blood sugar levels in a dog with diabetes. Considering that sugar is released into the blood after eating, your dog's diet must be carefully balanced. It is recommended that dogs with diabetes should eat a low-fat diet that is high in dietary fiber (Teixeira & Brunetto, 2017).

Kidney Disease: The waste products from protein metabolism are excreted through the kidneys. Therefore, dogs with kidney disease may require a low-protein diet rich in high-quality protein sources (Pedrinelli et al., 2020).

Liver Disease: Dogs suffering from liver disease require a low-protein diet using chicken and turkey as the main protein sources. The diet should also be low in copper, and high in antioxidants (Center, 2023).

Heart Disease: The diet of dogs with heart conditions should be low in sodium (salt) and potassium (found in foods such as potatoes, bananas, spinach, and legumes) (Freeman, n.d.).

Arthritis and Joint Issues: If your dog has joint issues, they may benefit from adding omega-3, glucosamine, and chondroitin supplements to their diet (Musco et al., 2019).

Cancer: Dogs undergoing cancer treatment may require diets to support their immune system, reduce inflammation, and maintain weight (Kramer et al., 2023).

Diet Plans Based on Activity Levels

The more active your dog, the more calories they need to con-sume. On the other hand, if your dog is a couch potato and keeps you company under your desk as you work all day, they may need you control how much they eat to avoid weight gain.

Use the activity factors detailed in chapter 1 to calculate your dog's energy requirements. A very active working dog can need to eat up to 5 times their MER, while an elderly sedentary dog only needs to consume 1.4 times their MER.

The exact nutrient requirements depend on the type of work or activity your dog does. For example, sled-pulling dogs need a higher fat intake, while racing Greyhounds need a higher protein intake to reduce the risk of anemia (Bermingham et al., 2014).

Sensitive Stomach

Think about the type of food you eat when your stomach is feel-ing a bit sensitive. People generally opt for foods that are gentle on the digestive system and easy to digest. Your dog with a sensi-tive stomach requires the same dietary considerations.

Your vet may suggest a bland diet consisting of chicken and rice for pets with acute digestive issues until they are able to toler-ate their normal diet again. You can also include foods, such as pureed pumpkin, shredded chicken or turkey, bone broth, and additive-free baby food. Such a meal ensures that you avoid com-mon food allergens, additives, and fillers that can irritate the gut (Burke, 2021).

Hypoallergenic

For dogs that have an adverse reaction to a variety of foods, it is crucial to identify the ingredients that trigger their immune system. The most common food ingredients causing allergies in dogs include proteins in beef, chicken, lamb, dairy products, and wheat (Mueller et al., 2016).

These should be the first foods you eliminate from their diet when trying to identify food allergens. However, there may be other ingredients your dog reacts to. It may be useful to avoid the foods you give them most often and reintroduce them one at a time to see whether their symptoms are triggered.

Once you know which foods to avoid, you can plan your furry friend's diet to accommodate their dietary restrictions. It's important to ensure that the diet is still nutritionally balanced. If your dog has several food allergies, it is advisable to consult your veterinarian for dietary advice.

Weight Management

Overweight and obesity can shorten your dog's lifespan and affect their quality of life. It also predisposes them to health conditions such as osteoarthritis, diabetes, and certain types of tumors, both cancerous and benign (German, 2016).

Research shows that high-protein diets with high fiber content are beneficial for weight management in dogs. The protein content should be greater than 30% of your dog's daily calorie requirements (Buff et al., 2014).

Talk to Your Veterinarian About Your Dog's Special Dietary Requirements

Whether your dog is overweight, extremely active, suffers from allergies or digestive issues, or has been diagnosed with a health condition, you must consult with a veterinarian about special diet options.

All these factors contribute to their dietary requirements. In some cases, if your dog eats too much of certain types of food, it may worsen their problem, and in others, too little of specific food ingredients or calories may harm them.

Homemade dog food makes it simple to adapt your dog's diet to meet their health-related needs. By tweaking the ingredients in the recipes you use, you can increase or reduce the problem foods to ensure your pet lives a longer, healthier life.

CONCLUSION

Your dog can't wait to say goodbye to boring old kibble forever and start devouring the delicious homemade meals you are going to start cooking for them. Finally, those enticing aromas wafting from the kitchen when you are preparing dinner might just be intended for their belly.

Canine nutrition is complex. There are several important factors to consider when deciding how much and what type of food your dog needs to eat. Everything from their breed to their size and from their age to their activity level must be included in their calorie requirement calculation.

Once you've wrapped your head around the complicated math equations, or if it makes your head spin, referred to the table of average calorie requirements for dogs, you must choose the recipes that will best meet your dog's nutrient requirements and unique food preferences.

From there, it's time to go shopping for the ingredients you plan to use for your homemade dog food. To ensure a healthy dog, it's best to buy the highest quality ingredients you can afford. That doesn't mean you have to break the bank. It simply means choosing whole foods that have been minimally processed and are free from additives, preservatives, and fillers.

Your dog will welcome the new variety in their diet. Even though they still gets excited when you put down a bowl full of kibble, they know there is so much more in your kitchen for them to taste.

Try to keep the food interesting for your pooch. When you feed them a range of different dishes, made from a variety of interesting ingredients, not only will it tempt their taste buds, but it will help ensure their nutrient intake is complete.

It's equally critical to practice good food hygiene to avoid food-borne illnesses in your dog. The last thing you want is for your carefully selected meals to make your pet sick. It's therefore important to buy the freshest ingredients you can and store their food safely in the fridge or freezer.

Remember that a sudden change in diet can adversely affect your pet. Take your time to plan and cook their meals and introduce the new food to your dog slowly over time. It usually takes about a week to transition your dog from their traditional dog food diet to a homemade dog food diet.

There may be bumps along the way that extend the timeline, but with a little patience and the willingness to adapt your meal plan, your dog will be enjoying their new diet before you know it.

No matter how carefully you research your dog's nutritional requirements and how much time you spend calculating, planning, and cooking, it is highly recommended that you consult with a veterinarian before transitioning to a homemade dog food diet.

The vet can advise you on any special requirements you must consider for your dog and recommend any nutritional supplements you may need to ensure that your dog's diet is well balanced and won't cause any nutritional excesses or deficiencies.

Continue to monitor your dog's progress throughout the transition period and for the first year on a homemade dog food diet. That way, the vet will be able to identify any new diet-related health issues before they become a problem and give you advice on how to adapt your dog's diet to remedy the deficiency or excess.

Your dog is an important member of your family and deserves to eat a healthy, nutritious, homemade diet. Now you can use what you have learned to calculate your dog's daily calorie requirements and create a wholesome meal plan for your furry best friend, using the recipes shared in this book.

Your homemade dog food creations will get your dog's mouth watering and their tail wagging. So, don your apron, take out the pots and pans, and start chopping, grating, boiling, baking, and mashing. Your dog will think you are a creative genius and the best chef in the world. Get ready for appreciative wet kisses!

If you've journeyed with me to the final page, thank you for your time and companionship along the way! Your readership is greatly appreciated, and it would be wonderful to hear your thoughts.

If you could spare a few moments to leave a review, it would not only help me to improve the storytelling but also assist fellow readers in finding their next great read.

Whether it's a few words of feedback or a detailed critique, all of your insights are invaluable. Thank you once again for choosing my book, and I hope to see you on the pages of one of my other books.

Warm regards,

Jamie

REFERENCES

Bakke, A. M., Wood, J., Salt, C., Allaway, D., Gilham, M., Kuhlman, G., Bierer, T., Butterwick, R., & O'Flynn, C. (2022). Responses in randomised groups of healthy, adult Labrador retrievers fed grain-free diets with high legume inclusion for 30 days display commonalities with dogs with suspected dilated cardiomyopathy. *BMC Veterinary Research*, *1*. https://doi.org/10.1186/s12917-022-03264-x

Bauer, J. J. E. (2008). Essential fatty acid metabolism in dogs and cats. *Revista Brasileira de Zootecnia*, *spe*, 20–27. https://doi.org/10.1590/s1516-35982008001300004

Bermingham, E. N., Thomas, D. G., Cave, N. J., Morris, P. J., Butterwick, R. F., & German, A. J. (2014). Energy Requirements of Adult Dogs: A Meta-Analysis. *PLoS ONE*, *10*, e109681. https://doi.org/10.1371/journal.pone.0109681

Buff, P. R., Carter, R. A., Bauer, J. E., &Kersey, J. H. (2014). Natural pet food: A review of natural diets and their impact on canine and feline physiology. *Journal of Animal Science*, *9*, 3781–3791. https://doi.org/10.2527/jas.2014-7789

Burke, A. (2021, June 10). *Five Foods to Feed Dogs With Upset Stomachs – American Kennel Club*. American Kennel Club; American Kennel Club. https://www.akc.org/expert-advice/nutrition/food-for-dogs-stomach-upset/

Callon, M. C., Cargo-Froom, C., DeVries, T. J., &Shoveller, A. K. (2017). Canine Food Preference Assessment of Animal and Vegetable Ingredient-Based Diets Using Single-Pan Tests and Behavioral Observation. *Frontiers in Veterinary Science*. https://doi.org/10.3389/fvets.2017.00154

Center, S. A. (2023, August 4). *Nutrition in Hepatic Disease in Small Animals - Digestive System - MSD Veterinary Manual*. MSD Veterinary Manual; MSD Veterinary Manual. https://www.msdvetmanual.

com/digestive-system/hepatic-diseases-of-small-animals/nutrition-in-hepatic-disease-in-small-animals

Cortinovis, C., &Caloni, F. (2016). Household Food Items Toxic to Dogs and Cats. *Frontiers in Veterinary Science*. https://doi.org/10.3389/fvets.2016.00026

Cridge, H., Lim, S. Y., Algül, H., & Steiner, J. M. (2022). New insights into the etiology, risk factors, and pathogenesis of pancreatitis in dogs: Potential impacts on clinical practice. *Journal of Veterinary Internal Medicine, 3*, 847–864. https://doi.org/10.1111/jvim.16437

da Costa, J. C., Coe, J. B., Blois, S. L., & Stone, E. A. (2022). Twenty-five components of a baseline, best-practice companion animal physical exam established by a panel of experts. *Journal of the American Veterinary Medical Association, 8*, 923–930. https://doi.org/10.2460/javma.21.10.0468

Davies, R. H., Lawes, J. R., & Wales, A. D. (2019). Raw diets for dogs and cats: a review, with particular reference to microbiological hazards. *Journal of Small Animal Practice, 6*, 329–339. https://doi.org/10.1111/jsap.13000

Dodd, S., Khosa, D., Dewey, C., &Verbrugghe, A. (2022). Owner perception of health of North American dogs fed meat- or plant-based diets. *Research in Veterinary Science*, 36–46. https://doi.org/10.1016/j.rvsc.2022.06.002

Dog and Cat Calorie Calculator | OSU Veterinary Medical Center. (n.d.). Home | College of Veterinary Medicine. Retrieved September 12, 2023, from https://vet.osu.edu/vmc/companion/our-services/nutrition-support-service/basic-calorie-calculator#:~:text=(Resting%20Energy%20Requirements%20or%20RER,to%20estimate%20resting%20calorie%20needs.

Domínguez-Oliva, A., Mota-Rojas, D., Semendric, I., & Whittaker, A. L. (2023). The Impact of Vegan Diets on Indicators of Health in Dogs and Cats: A Systematic Review. *Veterinary Sciences, 1*, 52. https://doi.org/10.3390/vetsci10010052

Feuer, D. (2006). *Your Dog's Nutritional Needs: A Science-Based Guide for Pet Owners.* National Academies. https://nap.

nationalacademies.org/resource/10668/dog_nutrition_final_fix.pdf

Fontaine, E. (2012). Food Intake and Nutrition During Pregnancy, Lactation and Weaning in the Dam and Offspring. *Reproduction in Domestic Animals*, s6, 326–330. https://doi.org/10.1111/rda.12102

Freeman, Dr. (n.d.). *Nutrition – HeartSmart*. HeartSmart – Information on Pets with Heart Disease. Retrieved October 12, 2023, from https://heartsmart.vet.tufts.edu/nutrition/

German, A. J. (2016). Weight management in obese pets: the tailoring concept and how it can improve results. *Acta Veterinaria Scandinavica*, S1. https://doi.org/10.1186/s13028-016-0238-z

German, A. J., Woods, G. R. T., Holden, S. L., Brennan, L., & Burke, C. (2018). Dangerous trends in pet obesity. *Veterinary Record*, 1, 25–25. https://doi.org/10.1136/vr.k2

Healthy Eating, Food Exchange Lists. (n.d.). Advancing Heart, Lung, Blood, and Sleep Research & Innovation | NHLBI, NIH. Retrieved September 27, 2023, from https://www.nhlbi.nih.gov/health/educational/lose_wt/eat/fd_exch.htm

Johnson, L. N., Linder, D. E., Heinze, C. R., Kehs, R. L., & Freeman, L. M. (2015). Evaluation of owner experiences and adherence to home-cooked diet recipes for dogs. *Journal of Small Animal Practice*, 1, 23–27. https://doi.org/10.1111/jsap.12412

Kramer, M. L., Larsen, J. A., & Kent, M. S. (2023). Changes in diet and supplement use in dogs with cancer. *Journal of Veterinary Internal Medicine*, 5, 1830–1838. https://doi.org/10.1111/jvim.16825

Liao, P., Yang, K., Huang, H., Xin, Z., Jian, S., Wen, C., He, S., Zhang, L., & Deng, B. (2023). Abrupt Dietary Change and Gradual Dietary Transition Impact Diarrheal Symptoms, Fecal Fermentation Characteristics, Microbiota, and Metabolic Profile in Healthy Puppies. *Animals*, 8, 1300. https://doi.org/10.3390/ani13081300

Montegiove, N., Calzoni, E., Cesaretti, A., Pellegrino, R. M., Emiliani, C., Pellegrino, A., & Leonardi, L. (2022). The Hard Choice about Dry Pet Food: Comparison of Protein and Lipid

Nutritional Qualities and Digestibility of Three Different Chicken-Based Formulations. *Animals, 12*, 1538. https://doi.org/10.3390/ani12121538

Mueller, R. S., Olivry, T., &Prélaud, P. (2016). Critically appraised topic on adverse food reactions of companion animals (2): common food allergen sources in dogs and cats. *BMC VeterinaryResearch, 1.* https://doi.org/10.1186/s12917-016-0633-8

Musco, N., Vassalotti, G., Mastellone, V., Cortese, L., della Rocca, G., Molinari, M. L., Calabrò, S., Tudisco, R., Cutrignelli, M. I., & Lombardi, P. (2019). Effects of a nutritional supplement in dogs affected by osteoarthritis. *Veterinary Medicine and Science, 3*, 325–335. https://doi.org/10.1002/vms3.182

Olivry, T., & Mueller, R. S. (2020). Critically appraised topic on adverse food reactions of companion animals (9): time to flare of cutaneous signs after a dietary challenge in dogs and cats with food allergies. *BMC VeterinaryResearch, 1.* https://doi.org/10.1186/s12917-020-02379-3

Pedrinelli, V., Lima, D. M., Duarte, C. N., Teixeira, F. A., Porsani, M., Zarif, C., Amaral, A. R., Vendramini, T. H. A., Kogika, M. M., & Brunetto, M. A. (2020). Nutritional and laboratory parameters affect the survival of dogs with chronic kidney disease. *PLOS ONE, 6*, e0234712. https://doi.org/10.1371/journal.pone.0234712

Pet Food | FDA. (n.d.). U.S. Food and Drug Administration. Retrieved September 16, 2023, from https://www.fda.gov/animal-veterinary/animal-food-feeds/pet-food

Rankovic, A., Adolphe, J. L., &Verbrugghe, A. (2019). Role of carbohydrates in the health of dogs. *Journal of the American Veterinary Medical Association, 5*, 546–554. https://doi.org/10.2460/javma.255.5.546

Recipe Calorie and Nutrition Calculator. (n.d.). Verywell Fit. Retrieved October 8, 2023, from https://www.verywellfit.com/recipe-nutrition-analyzer-4157076

Roberts, M. T., Bermingham, E. N., Cave, N. J., Young, W., McKenzie, C. M., & Thomas, D. G. (2017). Macronutrient intake of dogs, self-selecting diets varying in composition offered ad libitum. *Journal of Animal Physiology and Animal Nutrition*, 2, 568–575. https://doi.org/10.1111/jpn.12794

Staff. (2022, March 2). *How to Switch Dog Foods: Transitioning Your Dog's Diet*. American Kennel Club; American Kennel Club. https://www.akc.org/expert-advice/nutrition/right-way-switch-dog-foods/

Teixeira, F. A., & Brunetto, M. A. (2017). Nutritional factors related to glucose and lipid modulation in diabetic dogs: literature review. *Brazilian Journal of Veterinary Research and Animal Science*, 4, 330–341. https://doi.org/10.11606/issn.1678-4456.bjvras.2017.133289

Tizard, I. R. (2018, June 14). *Disorders Involving Anaphylactic Reactions (Type I Reactions, Atopy) in Dogs - Dog Owners - MSD Veterinary Manual*. MSD Veterinary Manual; MSD Veterinary Manual. https://www.msdvetmanual.com/dog-owners/immune-disorders-of-dogs/disorders-involving-anaphylactic-reactions-type-i-reactions,-atopy-in-dogs

WSAVA Global Nutrition Committee. (2020, July). *Calorie Ranges for an Average Healthy Adult Dog in Ideal Body Condition.*. Weave. Org. https://wsava.org/wp-content/uploads/2020/07/Calorie-Needs-for-Healthy-Adult-Dogs-updated-July-2020.pdf

Zanghi, B. M., & Gardner, C. L. (2018). Total Water Intake and Urine Measures of Hydration in Adult Dogs Drinking Tap Water or a Nutrient-Enriched Water. *Frontiers in Veterinary Science*. https://doi.org/10.3389/fvets.2018.00317

Made in United States
Troutdale, OR
02/03/2024

17431118R00095